THE FIRST CENTURY
OF ITALIAN HUMANISM

LANDMARKS IN HISTORY

Edited by Bernadotte E. Schmitt

THE FIRST CENTURY
OF
ITALIAN HUMANISM

BY

FERDINAND SCHEVILL
The University of Chicago

NEW YORK
F. S. CROFTS & CO.
1928

MANUFACTURED IN THE UNITED STATES OF AMERICA
BY THE VAIL-BALLOU PRESS, INC., BINGHAMTON, N. Y.

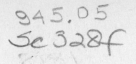
PREFACE TO SERIES

The use of "source books" in college classes in history is a well-established practice. Most of the source books now available, however, cover a long period of time, and their contents consist chiefly of single extracts illustrating specific incidents or describing social and economic conditions; it is rarely possible with the material thus provided to study any topic satisfactorily. In recent years a new type of source book has appeared which provides a series of problems, each of which is set forth in considerable detail and often with conflicting evidence. But usually the problems are so long that only one or two of them can be used in a single course; moreover, the number of problems offered is small, and only a few aspects of history are covered.

The purpose of *Landmarks in History* is to provide a number of problems of moderate length, each of which will be bound and sold separately. Extracts from the chief sources for the study of each problem will be put together in such a way as to illustrate at once the course of events and the forces at work and, at the same time, to give students a very fair idea of the materials from which history is written and of the methods of historical research. The problems will be short enough for several of them to be used during a year's course; the materials will be sufficiently varied to permit several kinds of exercises to be prepared; and the range of topics will, it is hoped, be wide enough to appeal to all kinds of tastes.

The series will cover the entire field of modern European history, from the Renaissance to the World War. A variety of problems are in active preparation, and it is planned to expand the list rapidly. In many cases source material in English translation will be made available for the first time. The co-operation of many well-known historians has been secured, and in general it may be said that each problem will be prepared by a scholar who has made a particular study of it.

These problems are offered to teachers of history with the conviction that they will supply a genuine need and that they will greatly facilitate that use of source materials, without which the teaching of history is likely to lose freshness and vitality.

BERNADOTTE E. SCHMITT

The University of Chicago

CONTENTS

HISTORICAL INTRODUCTION

This is a study in intellectual history and, more particularly, in the intellectual history of Italy during the one hundred to one hundred and twenty-five years between, let us say, 1325 and 1450 A.D. During this period there began to define itself quite clearly a new attitude toward life which the documents incorporated in this little volume offer an opportunity to explore.

It will be well if the student understands at the outset that intellectual change, such as is investigated here, is always an element in general cultural change, and that cultural change goes on in every civilized society uninterruptedly and at all times though at a variable pace. The Middle Age, which lies behind the first century of humanism and leads up to it, is still sometimes spoken of as if it had been, exceptionally, a period of cultural stagnation. This is of course absurd, for if its very leisurely unfolding may look like stagnation when compared with, say, the uniquely accelerated movement of the twentieth century, the age was nonetheless marked, within established limits, by numerous far-reaching changes. If, in view of this ceaseless flow, we are in the present instance singling out for study the change that came over men's thoughts in the course of the fourteenth century, it is because the novel ideas of that age very patently transcended the boundaries which had hitherto commanded universal respect, and by breaking them down, on the one hand, prepared the end of the Middle

Age and, on the other, assembled the raw materials destined to serve as the foundation of the new, the Modern Period. The first century of Italian humanism brought with it enough change in the outlook of men on life to constitute a crisis which may without impropriety be defined as a revolution.

Having agreed on cultural change at a variable rate as an established feature of civilization, we are logically prompted to inquire into its causes. This is an important issue, widely in debate at this very time, as it happens, among historians and sociologists, and indeed so complicated in its numerous and often hidden elements that it is out of the question to do justice to it here. Let it suffice to declare that intellectual change, that segment of cultural change which constitutes our immediate theme, must under no circumstances be supposed to rest exclusively on intellectual pre-conditions and postulates and to derive from a particularly vigorous effort of abstract thought. Were this the case, our ideas, having been produced in a vacuum, would have to be supposed to continue to exist in one—a more ridiculous assumption than which it would be difficult to imagine. The main thing to see and see clearly is that all thought movements are preëminently *social* and occur in close connection with every other agency to the action of which society is exposed and by which it is pushed forward on its path.

The process by which new ideas come to the front in a social milieu may be broadly indicated by the following general scheme. A society—any society—at a given moment of its evolution is endowed with a particular social-economic organization. With this goes an appropriate political government and a definite body of civil and criminal law. The religion and philosophy that flourish under these circumstances are highly important; and hardly less so, if at all, is the self-expression which the group under analysis achieves in literature and the fine arts. Now either by being brought into contact with other rival cultures, or by the breakdown of the social order at a particular point, or by the stimulus supplied by creative individuals, or in a score of other ways, the society of which we have supposed ourselves to be examining a cross-section is attacked from within and without and forced to alter its structure in order to survive under the new conditions. And any change in social structure brings with it a strictly corresponding change in thought, or, to put it another way, gives birth to a new religious and philosophic outlook.

To apply this formula of typical causation to the society here under consideration we must recall that the first century of Italian humanism was preceded by what we may conceive as the last phase of the Middle Age. Let us take this phase as covering essentially the thirteenth century with perhaps the first quarter of the fourteenth century thrown in (1200–1325 A.D.) and as reaching its highest imaginative expression in the Florentine poet, Dante Alighieri (d. 1321). As we all know, this age possessed a characteristic social-economic organization, government, and legal institutions together with a noble and appropriate expression in the arts and an impressive religio-philosophic outlook. Every aspect of the age is reflected as in a slowly revolving mirror in Dante's great poem, the *Divine Comedy*. The event, which was central to all else that took place, was without doubt the resumption of commercial and cultural contact with the Levant; and it was the curiously mixed company of crusaders, adventurers, and traders pouring into the Levant which caused goods and influences to

flow again between East and West. Then, having quick-
ened the life of the Mediterranean basin, the enterprising
spirits, chiefly merchants, began to push the nose of their
daring galleys into the uncharted waters of the Atlantic.
Under these broadening activities, throughout the Mediterranean area and, more particularly, in its Italian heart
and center, old towns were reborn and new ones came
to birth which with every new decade added to their
population, their wealth, and their power. An immediate
consequence was that new social classes took shape, while
old classes fell into subdivisions in conformity with the
many new occupations born of the commercial and in-
dustrial revival. Everywhere the *novi homines,* the merchants, filled with a vigorous self-consciousness, rose
against the baronial class who had exercised political
power under the older order of feudalism; and again, before long, the lower elements of the urban population rose
against the purse-proud merchants in the eager hope of
securing for themselves a share in the ever widening
economic opportunities. In sum, never since the days of
ancient Hellas had towns been so charged and overflow-
ing with vigor as, during this stirring period, the reborn
cities of Italy.

Presently the intellectual effect of all this movement
announced itself in the circumstance that men felt inspired
to enumerate and classify the new data of experience
to the end of acquiring a fuller mastery of the disturbing
situation. To feel and act in this manner meant, in the
last analysis, to have recourse to our human intelligence,
or, as the men of that age preferred to say, to our
reason or *ratio*. Essentially, too, the innovators gained
their point. Not that reason was permitted to go so far as
to challenge the Christian faith, for faith, ascribed to a
direct revelation from God, was held to be mandatory

and sacrosanct. Nevertheless reason was given the right to play a modest part in conjunction with and under the direction of faith; and on these terms a remarkable philosophic development took place known as scholasticism and reaching its most perfect formulation in St. Thomas Aquinas (d. 1274). Under this compromise, which asserted in unequivocal terms the continued primacy of Christianity and the Church, men retained their medieval outlook and yet rejoiced in the qualified use and freedom of their minds.

But the more courageous thinkers could not for long be held to the marriage of faith and reason on the simple ground that social change, revolving around the expanding city life, continued without interruption. There was an ever increasing trade, a larger production and greater diversity of goods, a widening circle of political unrest and experimentation, in short, a constantly waxing attachment to the problems growing out of active and exploratory living in the world. Unconsciously at first, and then with gradually awakening consciousness, men turned from the medieval absorption in the problem of salvation, which tended to withdraw them from life and make them other-worldly, to the task of making themselves more fully at home on a friendly earth. And it is here that the term humanism comes in. Humanism (from the Latin *homo, humanitas*) accurately registers the growing concern of men with themselves in their ephemeral mundane state; and since humanism came to a definite expression for the first time in Petrarch, Petrarch is often and not improperly called not only the first humanist but also the first modern man.

The selections in this book represent utterances of Petrarch and his followers during a period of a little over a hundred years. While it is left to the student to work out their significance for himself, it may not be amiss to point out to him certain lines of profitable inquiry:

(a) These early Italian humanists were all passionate champions of antiquity, at bottom for no other reason than that the classical authors by disclosing the highly developed secular civilization of Greece and Rome provided the novelty-seeking Italians not only with a point of reference and guidance but also—a very important matter in view of the overwhelming authority of the Church—with a moral and intellectual sanction for the independent course they steered.

(b) Filled with fresh curiosity in the human scene, the humanists became closely attentive to nature, took to travel for its own sake, and developed their powers of accurate observation.

(c) On the purely intellectual side they recognized scholasticism, ensconced in both the Church and the universities, as the immediate enemy and tried in every way to discredit it.

(d) Though they bowed to the authority of the Church as an institution, and in the main continued to reverence Christianity, they became very critical of the ministers and servants of the Church, the clergy.

(e) Recognizing that their new secular viewpoint called for a revised training of youth, they proposed and achieved a new curriculum, new teaching methods, and a new educational spirit.

These general directions taken in connection with the Exercises and the Questions at the end of the book should enable the student to extract from the documents every significant trait of the first phase of the intellectual movement called humanism.

LIST OF THE HUMANISTS WHOSE WRITINGS ARE UTILIZED IN THIS STUDY

Francesco Petrarca (Petrarch), 1304–74
Giovanni Boccaccio, 1313–75
Coluccio Salutati, 1331–1406
Pietro Paolo Vergerio, 1349–1419
Leonardo Bruni of Arezzo, 1369–1444
Poggio Bracciolini, 1380–1459
Aeneas Silvius Piccolomini (Pope Pius II), 1405–1464
Lorenzo Valla, 1406–57
Vespasiano da Bisticci, 1421–98
Battista Guarino, 1434–1500 (?)

DATA ON SOURCES

As most of the sources are in Latin and are exceedingly rare because they have not been reprinted for centuries, it has been considered desirable to refer the reader, in addition to the more accessible Latin editions, to translations into English and, in default of an English rendering, to translations into other European languages.

Petrarch. *Opera.* Printed at Basel in 1581. Imperfect, but to date the most complete collection of Petrarch's works in existence.

Petrarch. *Epistolae de rebus familiaribus et variae.* Edited by Fracassetti. 3 vols. Florence, 1859–63. This edition supplies a revised Latin text for the largest of the several collections of Petrarch's letters.

Petrarch. *Lettere delle cose familiari e lettere varie.* The above letters translated into Italian by G. Fracassetti. 5 vols. Florence. 1863–67.

Petrarch. *Lettere senili.* Translated into Italian by G. Fracassetti. 2 vols. Florence. 1892.

Petrarch. *Letters to Classical Authors.* Translated from the Latin with a commentary by Mario Cosenza. The University of Chicago Press. 1910.

Petrarch. *Lettres à Boccace.* Traduites par V. Develay. Paris. 1891.

Petrarch. *The First Modern Scholar and Man of Letters.* A Selection from his Correspondence . . . translated from the original Latin by James H. Robinson,

8

with the collaboration of Henry W. Rolfe. New York. 1898.

Petrarch. *The Secret or the Soul's Conflict with Passion*. Three Dialogues between the Author and St. Augustine. Translated from the Latin by William H. Draper. London. 1911.

Boccaccio. *Il Decameron*. There exist innumerable Italian editions and several English translations. A readable translation is that of W. K. Kelly. London. Bohn's Library.

Salutati. *Epistolario di Coluccio Salutati a cura di Francesco Novati*. 4 vols. Rome. 1891–1911.

Emerton, Ephraim. *Humanism and Tyranny*. Studies in the Italian Trecento. Harvard University Press. 1925. Contains a translation of some letters of Salutati in defense of liberal studies together with an admirable introduction by the translator.

Gratius, Orthuinus. *Fasciculus rerum* etc. Edited by Edward Brown. London. 1690. Contains the letter written by Poggio to his Florentine fellow-humanist, Leonardo Bruni, regarding the trial and condemnation of Jerome of Prague in 1416.

Whitcomb, Merrick. *A Literary Source-Book of the Italian Renaissance*. The University of Pennsylvania. 1898. Contains, in translation, selections from many humanists.

Muratori. *Rerum Italicarum Scriptores*. Vol. XIX. Milan, 1731. Contains Leonardo Bruni's History of his own Times.

Poggio Bracciolini. *The Facetiae or Jocose Tales of Poggio*. Now first translated into English with the Latin Text. 2 vols. Paris. Isidore Liseux. 1879.

Der Briefwechsel des Eneas Silvius Piccolomini. Herausgegeben von Rudolf Wolkan. Fontes Rerum Austriacarum. II Abtheilung. Bände LXI, LXII, LXVII. III Abtheilung. Band I. Vienna. 1909–18.

Mell, Max. *Enea Silvio Piccolomini Briefe.* (Das Zeitalter der Renaissance: Ausgewählte Quellen zur Geschichte der Italienischen Kultur. Herausgegeben von Marie Herzfeld.) Eugen Diederichs. Jena. 1911. A scholarly introduction is followed by a German rendering of forty-three characteristic letters.

Coleman, Christopher B. *The Treatise of Lorenzo Valla on the Donation of Constantine.* Text and Translation into English. New Haven. Yale University Press. 1922.

Vespasiano da Bisticci. *Vite di Uomini Illustri del Secolo XV.* Florence. 1859.

The Vespasiano Memoirs. *Lives of Illustrious Men of the XVth Century.* By Vespasiano da Bisticci, Bookseller. Now first translated into English by William George and Emily Waters. London, 1926.

Woodward, William H. *Vittorino da Feltre and Other Humanist Educators.* An Introduction to the History of Classical Education. Cambridge. At the University Press. 1905. An excellent analysis and review of the New Education together with an English translation of the treatises of four educators and educational theorists, Pietro Paolo Vergerio, Leonardo Bruni, Aeneas Silvius Piccolomini, and Battista Guarino.

CONVENIENT WORKS OF REFERENCE DEALING WITH ITALIAN HUMANISM

Symonds, John A. *The Renaissance in Italy.* 7 vols. Vol. II "The Revival of Learning." New York. Henry Holt and Company.

Hulme, E. M. *The Renaissance, the Protestant Revolution and the Catholic Reformation in Continental Europe.* New York. The Century Co. 1917.

Emerton, E. *The Beginnings of Modern Europe (1250–1450).* Particularly Chapters VIII and IX. Boston. Ginn and Company.

Monnier, Philippe. *Le Quattrocento.* Essai sur L'Histoire Littéraire du XV Siècle Italien. 2 vols. Lausanne. Payot et Cie.

Geiger, Ludwig. *Renaissance und Humanismus in Italien und Deutschland.* Berlin. Grote'scher Verlag.

Voigt, Georg. *Die Wiederbelebung des classischen Alterthums.* 2 vols. Berlin. Georg Reimer.

Nolhac, Pierre de. *Petrarch and the Ancient World.* Boston. The Merrymount Press. 1907.

Nolhac, Pierre de. *Petrarque et l'Humanisme.* 2 vols. Paris. Champion.

Hollway Calthorp, H. G. *Petrarch, His Life and Times.* New York. Putnam. 1907.

Tatham, E. H. R. *Francesco Petrarca. The First Modern Man of Letters.* 2 vols. London. The Sheldon Press. 1925.

Boulting, W. *Aeneas Silvius (Pius II) Orator, Man of Letters, Statesman, Pope.* London. Constable. 1908.

Burckhardt, J. C. *The Civilization of the Renaissance in Italy.* Translated by S. G. Middlemore. London. Allen and Unwin.

Gebhart, E. *Les Origines de la Renaissance en Italie.* Paris. 1879.

Sandys, John E. *A History of Classical Scholarship.* 3 vols. Vol. II deals with the Renaissance. Cambridge. At the University Press.

THE SOURCES

PART I. NEW MENTAL INTERESTS; PERSISTENCE OF
OLD MENTAL INTERESTS

a) *Extracts from the Letters of Petrarch*

1. Two Letters to Cardinal Giovanni Colonna, dated
Aachen, June 21, 1333, and Lyons, August 9, 1333.
De Rebus Familiaribus, ed. Fracassetti, 1, 3, 4.
Robinson and Rolfe, *Petrarch,* p. 298 ff.

I have lately been traveling through France, not on
business, as you know, but simply from a youthful curiosity to see the country. I finally penetrated into Germany
to the banks of the Rhine itself. I have carefully noted
the customs of the people and have been much interested
in observing the characteristics of a country hitherto un-
known to me and in comparing the things I saw with
those at home. While I found much to admire in both
countries, I in no way regretted my Italian origin. (*He
mentions his sojourn in Paris, Ghent, Liège, and Aachen.*)
I then proceded to Cologne, which lies on the left bank
of the Rhine and is noted for its situation, its river, and
its inhabitants. I was astonished to find such a degree of
culture in a barbarous land. The appearance of the city,
the dignity of the men, the attractiveness of the women,
all surprised me. The day of my arrival happened to be
the feast of St. John the Baptist. It was nearly sunset
when I reached the city. On the advice of the friends,
whom my reputation rather than any true merit had

won for me even there, I allowed myself to be led immediately from the inn to the river to witness a curious sight. And I was not disappointed for I found the river-bank lined with a multitude of remarkably comely women. . . .

I took my stand upon a little rise of ground where I could easily follow what was going on. There was a dense mass of people but no disorder of any kind. They knelt down in quick succession on the bank, half-hidden by the fragrant grass, and turning up their sleeves above the elbow they bathed their hands and white arms in the eddying stream. . . . Not understanding the scene and being deeply interested in it, I asked an explanation from one of my friends. . . . He told me that this was an old custom among the people and that the lower classes, especially the women, have the greatest confidence that the threatening calamities of the coming year can be washed away by bathing on this day in the river and a happier fate be so assured. . . .

During the few days following I wandered about the city under the guidance of my friends from morning until night. I enjoyed these rambles not so much for what I actually saw as on account of the reminiscences of our ancestors, who have left such extraordinary monuments to the Roman power in this far-distant country. . . . I saw, too, the great church (*the Cologne Cathedral*) in the very center of the town. It is very beautiful, although still uncompleted, and is not unjustly regarded by the inhabitants as the finest building of its kind in the world. I looked with reverence upon the relics of the Three Kings, who, as we read, came once upon a time, bringing presents, to worship at the feet of a Heavenly King as he lay wailing in the manger. Their bodies were brought from the East to the West in three great leaps.[1] (*The bodies were currently believed to have been carried first to Constantinople, then to Milan, and finally to Cologne.*)

2. Letter to Thomas of Messina, dated Avignon, March 11, 1335 (?). *De Rebus Familiaribus,* ed. Fracassetti, I, 6; Robinson and Rolfe, *Petrarch,* p. 217 ff.

(*To appreciate this letter the reader should remember that education in Petrarch's day was still built around the medieval curriculum, somewhat grandiloquently called the Seven Liberal Arts. It was composed of two sections, the trivium and quadrivium, of which the trivium was by far the more substantial. The trivium included grammar (Latin), rhetoric (composition), and logic (dialectic). During the scholastic century preceding Petrarch's birth logic had pressed to the front usurping the primacy which men like Petrarch claimed for grammar and rhetoric, the natural basis for an education of a more humanistic turn.*) You write to me of a certain old logician, who has been greatly excited by my letter as if I condemned his art. With a growl of rage he loudly threatened to make war in turn upon our studies in a letter for which, you say, you have waited many months in vain. Do not wait any longer, for, believe me, it will never come. . . .

These logicians seek to cover their teachings with the splendor of Aristotle's name. They claim that Aristotle was wont to argue in the same way. . . . But they

[1] This and the three following selections from *Petrarch, The First Modern Scholar and Man of Letters,* by James H. Robinson and Henry W. Rolfe, are used by the courtesy of G. P. Putnam's Sons, Publishers, New York and London.

deceive themselves. Aristotle was a man of the most exalted genius, who not only discussed but wrote upon themes of the very highest importance. How can we otherwise explain so vast an array of his works, involving such prolonged labor and prepared with such supreme care? . . . Why is not the name of Aristotelians a source of shame to them rather than of satisfaction, for no one could be more utterly different from that great philosopher than a man who writes nothing, knows but little, and constantly indulges in much vain declamation? Who does not laugh at their trivial conclusions, with which they weary both themselves and others? They waste their whole lives in such contentions . . . We find an example in the case of Diogenes, whom a contentious logician addressed as follows: "What I am, you are not." Upon Diogenes conceding this, the logician added: "But I am a man." As this was not denied, the poor quibbler triumphantly offered the deduction: "Therefore you are not a man." "The last statement is not true," Diogenes remarked, "but if you wish it to be true, begin with me in your major premise." . . .

On hearing such jibes as these, the logicians grow furious: "So you set yourself up to condemn logic," they cry. Far from it. I know well in what esteem it was held by that sturdy and virile sect of philosophers, the Stoics. I know that it is one of the Seven Liberal Arts, a ladder for those who are striving upwards. It stimulates the intellect, points the way to truth, shows us how to avoid fallacies, and, finally, if it accomplishes nothing else, makes us ready and quick-witted.

All this I freely admit. But because a road is proper for us to travel, it does not follow that we should linger on it forever. . . . Dialectic may form a portion of our road; it is certainly not our goal.

3. Letter to Dionisio of Borgo San Sepolcro, dated
Malaucène, April 26, 1336. *De Rebus Familiari-
bus,* ed. Francassetti, IV, i; Robinson and Rolfe,
Petrarch, p. 307 ff.

Today I made the ascent of the highest mountain in
this region (*Vaucluse, France*) which is not improperly
called Ventosum (*Windy*). My only motive was to see
what so high an elevation had to offer. I have had the
expedition in mind for many years; for, as you know,
I have lived in this region from infancy, having been
cast here by that fate which determines the affairs of
men. Consequently the mountain, which is visible from
a great distance, was ever before my eyes, and I con-
ceived the plan of some time doing what I have at last
accomplished today. (*On casting about for a companion
he decides in favor of his younger brother, and the two
attended by two servants to carry the luggage travel to
the foot of the mountain where they pass the night. They
begin the ascent in the morning.*)
The mountain is a very steep and almost inaccessible
mass of stony soil. . . . It was a long day, the air fine.
We enjoyed the advantage of vigor of mind and strength
and agility of body and everything else essential to those
engaged in such an undertaking, and so had no other
difficulties to face than those of the region itself. We
found an old shepherd in one of the mountain dales who
tried at great length to dissuade us from the ascent,
saying that some fifty years before he had, in the same
ardor of youth, reached the summit, but had gotten for
his pains nothing except fatigue and regret, and clothes
and body torn by the rocks and briars. No one, so far
as he or his companions knew, had ever tried the ascent
before or after him. But his counsels increased rather than

diminished our desire to proceed since youth is impatient of warnings. So the old man, finding that his efforts were in vain, went a little way with us and pointed out a rough path among the rocks, uttering many admonitions which he continued to send after us even after we had left him behind. Surrendering to him all such garments or other possessions as might prove burdensome to us, we made ready for the ascent and started off at a good pace. (*The difficulties of the climb are described in some detail, in spite of which the peak is at last scaled.*)

At first, owing to the unaccustomed quality of the air and to the effect of the great sweep of view spread out before me, I stood like one dazed. I beheld the clouds under our feet, and what I had read of Athos and Olympus seemed less incredible as I myself witnessed the same things from a mountain of less fame. I turned my eyes toward Italy, whither my heart most inclined. The Alps, rugged and snow-capped, seemed to rise close by. . . . I sighed, I must confess, for the skies of Italy, which I beheld rather with my mind than with my eyes. An inexpressible longing came over me to see once more my friend and my country. . . . (*On turning to the West*) I could see with the utmost clearness, off to the right, the mountains of the region about Lyons, and to the left the bay of Marseilles and the waters that lash the shores of Aigues Mortes, although all these places were so distant that it would require a journey of several days to reach them. Under our very eyes flowed the Rhone.

While I was thus dividing my thoughts, now turning my attention to some terrestrial object that lay before me, now raising my soul, as I had done my body, to higher planes, it occurred to me to look into my copy of St. Augustine's Confessions, a gift that I owe to your love and that I always have about me in memory of both the author and the giver. I opened the compact little volume with the intention of reading whatever came to hand, for I could happen upon nothing that would be otherwise than edifying and devout. Now it chanced that the tenth book presented itself. My brother, waiting to hear something of St. Augustine's from my lips, stood attentively by. I call him, and God too, to witness that where I first fixed my eyes it was written: "And men go about to wonder at the heights of the mountains and the mighty waves of the sea and the wide sweep of the rivers and the circuit of the ocean and the revolution of the stars, but themselves they consider not." I was abashed and, asking my brother who was anxious to hear more, not to annoy me, I closed the book, angry with myself that I should still be admiring earthly things who might long ago have learned from even the pagan philosophers that nothing is wonderful but the soul, which, when great itself, finds nothing great outside itself. Then in truth I was satisfied that I had seen enough of the mountain; I turned my inward eye upon myself, and from that time not a syllable fell from my lips until we reached the bottom again.

4. Letter to Pulice of Vicenza, dated Near Vicenza, May 13, 1351. *De Rebus Familiaribus,* ed. Fracassetti, XXIV, 2; Robinson and Rolfe, *Petrarch,* p. 243 ff.

(The writer recalls a recent visit at the house of his correspondent in Vicenza, on which occasion the conversation of the assembled company of scholars had swung to Cicero. To every one's surprise Petrarch had ventured to intersperse amidst abundant praises a few criticisms

*of the Roman author and orator and, to clinch his point,
had fetched from among his baggage two letters to
Cicero which he had had composed as literary exercises
and in which he had enumerated Cicero's merits and de-
merits.)* These two (*letters*) you read while the others
listened; and then the strife of words grew warmer.
Some approved of what I had written, admitting that
Cicero deserved my censure. But the old man stood his
ground more stubbornly even than before. He was so
blinded by love of his hero and by the brightness of his
name that he preferred to praise him even when he was
in the wrong; to embrace faults and virtues together
rather than make any exceptions. He would not be
thought to condemn anything at all in so great a man.
So instead of answering our arguments he rang the
changes again and again upon the splendor of Cicero's
fame, letting authority usurp the place of reason. He
would stretch out his hand and say imploringly,
"Gently, I beg of you, gently with my Cicero." And
when we asked him if he found it impossible to believe
that Cicero had made mistakes, he would close his eyes
and turn his face away and exclaim with a groan, as if
he had been smitten, "Alas! alas! Is my beloved Cicero
accused of doing wrong?" just as if he were speaking
not of a man but of some god. I asked him accordingly
whether in his opinion Tullius was a god or a man like
others. "A god," he replied; and then realizing what he
had said, he added, "a god of eloquence."

5. Letter to Lapo of Castiglionchio, dated Avignon, April
    1, 1352. *De Rebus Fam.,* ed. Francassetti, XII, 8;
    Cosenza, *Petrarch's Letters to Classical Authors,*
    p. 39 ff.

According to my custom I fled recently from the turmoil of the city that is so odious to me and betook myself to my Helicon across the Alps (*i.e. to his country-home near Avignon. Not far away rose the mountain described in Letter 3*). I brought with me your Cicero, who was greatly astonished at the beauty of these new regions and who confessed that never—not even when in his own retreat at Arpinum—had he, to use his own phrase, been surrounded by cooler streams than when with me at the Fountain of the Sorgue. . . . This quiet, peaceful country and this delightful retreat are situated to one side of the public highway. . . . No mere passerby has ever discovered it. No one has ever reached it except purposing to do so through certain knowledge of its existence, drawn to the spot by the beauty of the fountain or by his desire for repose and study. . . . Cicero therefore seems to rejoice and to be eager to remain in my company. We have now passed ten quiet and restful days together here. Here only and in no other place outside Italy do I breathe freely. In truth, study has this great virtue that it appeases our desire for a life of solitude, mitigates our aversion for the vulgar herd, tenders us sought-for repose even in the midst of the thickest crowds, instills in us many noble thoughts, and provides us with the fellowship of illustrious men even in the most solitary forests. (*There follows an enumeration of the works of Cicero with which he has employed his time.*) With such men and others as my companions my stay in the country has been a quiet, peaceful, and happy one.[1]

---

[1] This selection from *Petrarch's Letters to Classical Authors,* by Mario E. Cosenza, is used by the courtesy of The University of Chicago Press.

6. Letter to Boccaccio, dated Milan, August 18, 1360.
Epistolae Variae, ed. Fracassetti, 25.

. . . Finally, believing that I have acquired the copy
of Homer which was for sale at Padua, you ask me to
lend it to you, and are encouraged to make your request by your knowledge that I have long been in possession of another copy. Your plan is to have your friend
Leo translate it from Greek into Latin for the benefit not
only of ourselves but of all our studious compatriots.
(*The Leo here referred to was a Greek of southern
Italy whom Boccaccio had taken into his house in order
to learn Greek from him.*) I saw this volume but I
neglected to buy it because it seemed to me inferior to
my own. It ought to be easy to get hold of through the
mediation of the person who procured for me the friend-
ship of Leo. A letter from the latter should clinch the
bargain, especially if I add my word. If by any chance
the volume should escape us—which I will not suppose
—I shall send you mine. For I have always been hungry
for a translation of Homer and indeed for Greek literature in general; and if fortune had not crossed my plans
by the untimely death of my excellent master [1] I would
possibly be something more today than a Greek who
is still at his alphabet. With all my heart and all my
strength I therefore second your enterprise, for I have
never ceased regretting that the ancient translation, which
seems to have been a labor of Cicero's and of which
Horace has inserted the opening passage in his *Ars
Poetica,* has, like so many other works, been lost to the
Latin world.

[1] A Greek by the name of Barlaham or Barlaam.

7. Letter to Boccaccio dated Venice, September 7, 1363.
   Fracassetti, *Lettere Senili*, III, 1.

(*After lamenting the death of two of his friends and
the ills which are assaulting the world he takes up the
pest of the diviners and astrologers, exhibiting a remarkable freedom from many of the superstitions of his age.
On the subject of astrologers he mixes criticism and
banter.*) Without doubt when they speak of the movements of the heavenly bodies, when they discuss the wind
and the rain, the heat and the cold, the storms of the
sea and the eclipses of the sun and moon, one may hear
them often with profit; but when they discourse on
human events which only God knows, they must needs
be rejected as weavers of frightful lies and be banished
from the society not only of the educated but of all
decent folk. By a strange twist in their minds and with
an astonishing obstinacy they neglect the possible and
abandon themselves to the impossible. (*He then turns
to an astrologer of Milan, a good fellow for the rest and
a friend of his, who was regularly employed by the Vis-
conti family, the rulers of Milan, in connection with all
their enterprises. No step of any consequence, above all,
no military expedition was undertaken before this man
had spoken his foolish word. Petrarch recounts two amus-
ing instances when the astrologer's prognostications proved
to be ludicrously wrong.*) In view of these circumstances
I have often twitted my prophetic friend, who invariably
answered me that he was no wiser than his art. I am
convinced he spoke the truth, and what excuses him somewhat is his age and the cruel necessity he is under of
bringing up a numerous family. That this is the reason
why he has given himself over to this hocus-pocus seems
to me to be proved by an answer he recently made me.

Really liking the man, I have often remonstrated with him, although he exceeds me both in years and indeed in knowledge. On one of these occasions, like a man aroused from sleep, he said to me with a sigh: "I think on these matters, dear friend, exactly like yourself. But a man must live!"

8. Letter to Boccaccio dated Pavia, December 10, 1364. Fracassetti, *Lettere Senili*, V, 3.

(*Boccaccio has reported that he has been ill but has recovered without calling a physician.*) I am not at all astonished that you recovered so quickly. The best cure for a sick man is to get rid of the doctor. That may sound queer to those who have not tried it but to those who have it is proved and certain.

The physicians boast that they are the helpers of nature. Often enough they fight against nature and on the side of disease. The least bad among them maintain a kind of neutrality, stand by and await the issue. (*He expresses the opinion that their ancestors, the Romans, in their best period got along without doctors, who are a foreign pest originating in Greece.*) Would that they really were doctors and not enemies of medicine operating under the label of doctors! They have descended among us equipped not only with their own ignorance but also with the folly and credulity of the sick tormented by so great a desire to be cured that whosoever with some measure of assurance holds out a promise of health looks to them like Apollo in person. And indeed the necessary assurance never fails any of them. They employ as an aid to their deception a most efficacious weapon: an impudence and self-assertion which the habit of lying has made imperturbable. Add to this a usurped costume, of which they are unworthy, consisting of a robe of purple with ornaments in various colors, sparkling rings, and gilded spurs, and now tell me, wouldn't even a man in full possession of his senses be overcome by such display? . . .

I know that there are many people who believe that I am the declared enemy of doctors on account of the resounding debate I once had with them in France. Aside from the fact that I have many friends among the physicians, this charge is in itself so absurd that it cannot be believed except of a fool or a madman. . . . In fact I love both the doctors and their art though I hate the quacks who, armed with a subtile dialectic, instead of effecting a cure overwhelm with boredom the people who are well and administer a veritable death-blow to the sick. These, I admit, whose numbers are legion, I hate; the former however, who are extremely rare, I love. . . .

Everything in medicine takes place in Greek or, what is even more disagreeable still, in Arabic, on the assumption that a lie which comes from a distance is more likely to be believed and that a foreign remedy commands a greater price. In consequence no sooner do the physicians enter the sick-room than they pronounce the Greek name of the disease, or, at need, invent it. This is, they say gravely, an epilepsy, or an apoplexy, or an erysipelas. Beautiful names, these, capable of giving delight to whoever hears them; only, the hearers are prompted to ask, why call that which a Latin suffers by a Greek name, seeing that the remedies are neither Latin nor Greek? But enough of these medical pleasantries.

9. Letter to Boccaccio dated Venice, August 28, 1366. Fracassetti, *Lettere Senili,* V, 2.

(*Petrarch begins this letter with a discussion of the*

Italian language and literature. But as he had been moved during his long life to direct his attention more and more to Latin, he draws this language into the debate.) Latin, in both prose and poetry, has been so thoroughly developed by the great authors of antiquity that it is almost impossible for anybody to add very much. Our language (*Italian*), on the other hand, has but recently been discovered, and though it has been devastated by many, it is cultivated by some serious workers and under their hands should greatly improve. Carried away by this thought and by the impulsiveness of youth, I began a considerable work in that language (*his famous Book of Songs?*). Having laid the foundations of the structure and got together my lime, stones, and wood, I began to consider a little more carefully the age in which we live, an age which is the mother of pride and indolence. I noted the profundity of the vain fellows round about me and their enunciation, which is so charming that they do not so much recite the writings of others as tear them to tatters. (*After enlarging on the incompetence of his contemporaries to appreciate the new Italian literature, he launches an attack on them for their uncomprehending attitude towards the classics.*)

O inglorious age, that despises antiquity, its mother, which invented every noble art! You even dare declare yourself not only equal but also superior to the past. I leave out of consideration the vulgar, the dregs of mankind, whose sayings and opinions deserve a laugh rather than serious censure. I will say nothing of the professional soldiers and their generals, who do not blush to assert that their time has seen the culmination of the military art, when the truth is that this art has utterly degenerated in their hands. . . . I will pass over the kings who act as if they thought that their office consisted of purple and gold, of scepter and diadem, and that they excelled the ancients in valor and glory. Elevated to the throne for the single purpose of exercising rule, they do not govern in any serious sense but, as their conduct shows, are themselves governed by their pleasures. However, their ignorance of antiquity may serve in some measure to excuse them. But, I ask, what excuse is there for men of education who ought to know the classics and yet are plunged in this same darkness?

I agree that I cannot speak of these matters without the greatest indignation. There has recently arisen a set of dialecticians who are not only ignorant but insane. Like a black army of ants from some rotten oak, they swarm forth and ravage the fields of sound learning. They condemn Plato and Aristotle, they laugh at Socrates and Pythagoras. . . . I have occasionally been present when Virgil, the sun of eloquence, was the subject of their censure. Astonished at their mad outbreak, I turned to a person of apparent education and asked what infamy he had detected in a man so celebrated. Here is the reply he gave me with a contemptuous shrug: "He throws his conjunctions around too freely." . . .

What shall I say of that other kind of pedant who wears a religious garb though most profane in heart and conduct, and dares affirm that Ambrose, Augustine, and Jerome were ignoramuses? I do not know the origin of these new theologians who do not respect the Holy Fathers and who will not much longer respect the Apostles and the Gospel unless He in person interferes and curbs the raging beasts. . . . Recently one of this ilk visited me in my library. True, he did not, like the others, wear a religious garb, but, after all, Christianity does not depend on clothes. He was, as I was saying, one of those who think they live in vain unless they are

constantly snapping at Christ and his divine teachings.
When I cited some passage or other from HolyWrit, he
burst forth, livid with rage: "Hug to your breast the
little doctors of the Church . . . Be a good Christian! As
for me I believe in none of that. Your Paul and your
Augustine and all the rest you preach about were a set of
babblers. If you would only read Averroes you would
quickly see how he towers above those triflers of yours." I
was angry, I must confess, and could scarcely keep from
striking his blasphemous mouth. "It is the old quarrel between me and you heretics," I said to him. "Go, and never
return, neither you nor your heresy!"

10. Letter to Boccaccio dated Padua, April 28, 1373.
Fracassetti, *Lettere Senili,* XVII, 20.

. . . Certainly I shall not reject the praise you bestow upon me for having aroused, not only in Italy but
also beyond its boundaries, a passion for these studies of
ours, neglected for so many centuries. I am almost the
oldest of all those engaged in their pursuit. But I reject
the conclusion you draw from this, to wit, that I should
give place to younger talents and, terminating my labors,
give others an opportunity to write, free from the fear
that it is my wish to monopolize everything for myself.
How greatly our opinions differ, although we have the
same desire at heart! It seems to you that I have written
everything, while in my own opinion I have produced
almost nothing. . . .

Work and application are my soul's best food. So
soon as ever I begin to rest and relax I shall cease to
live. I know my powers; I am not fitted for any other
kind of work. Reading and writing, which you would
have me renounce, are light work, nay, they are a sweet

repose, liberating me from my heavy anxieties. There is no lighter burden than a pen nor is there one more agreeable. Other pleasures abandon us or wound while they charm; but the pen is taken up with gladness and laid down with satisfaction, for it has the power to benefit not only him who wields it but many others as well, even those who are far away, sometimes even those who are born after thousands of years. I believe that I am speaking the truth when I declare that there is among earthly delights none more noble than literature. . . .

Pardon me then, my brother, pardon me. I am prepared to believe everything you say, but not this. Whatever you think of me, I must still endeavor, if I am nothing, to become something; if I am something, to become a little more; and if I am great—which I am not—to become, as far as lies in me, greater and even the greatest.

b) Extracts from Petrarch's "Secret"

11. Petrarch's Secret or The Soul's Conflict with Passion. Three Dialogues between Petrarch and St. Augustine. Translated from the Latin by William H. Draper.

(*No work of Petrarch's shows as strikingly as this to what degree the great pioneer, often called the first modern man, continued to be held enthralled by medieval concepts. Without doubt Petrarch's novel literary and secular activities often overwhelmed him with a sense of guilt. In this dialogue Petrarch tries weakly to defend his position but yields point after point to the spirited Augustine, who reasserts every essential feature of the medieval faith touching the emptiness of our life on this earth.*)

S. AUGUSTINE. Every one knows, and the greatest philosophers are of the same opinion, that of all tremendous realities death is the most tremendous. So true is this that from of old its very name is terrible and dreadful to hear. Yet though so it is, it will not do that we hear that name lightly, or allow the remembrance of it to slip quickly from our mind. We must take time to realize it. We must meditate with attention thereon. We must picture to ourselves the effect of death on each part of our bodily frame, the cold extremities, the breast in the sweat of fever, the side throbbing with pain, the eyes sunken and weeping, the forehead pale and drawn, the teeth staring and discolored, the lips foaming, the tongue foul and motionless, the evil smell of the whole body, the horror of seeing the face utterly unlike itself —all these things will come to mind and, so to speak, be ready to one's hand, if one recalls what he has seen in any close observation of some deathbed which it has fallen to his lot to attend. . . . This is what I mean by letting the thought of death sink deeply into the soul. Falling in with the evil custom of our time, you probably never name the name of death, although nothing is more certain than the fact or more uncertain than the hour. . . .

(*Having brought Petrarch to acknowledge the need of thinking upon death, he continues his inquisition.*)

S. AUGUSTINE. . . . You are charmed with the very chains that are dragging you to your death and, what is most sad of all, you glory in them!

PETRARCH. What may these chains be of which you speak?

S. AUGUSTINE. Love and glory.

PETRARCH. Great Heavens! What is this I hear? You call these things chains? And you would break them from me if I would let you?

S. AUGUSTINE. Yes, I mean to try; but I doubt if I shall succeed.

PETRARCH. (*He makes at considerable length a very noble defense of his love for Laura, who has inspired his verse and with whom his relationship has been pure and honorable.*)

S. AUGUSTINE. And now I shall deliver my sharpest thrust of all. In simple truth that woman, to whom you profess to owe everything, she, even she, has been your ruin.

PETRARCH. Good Heavens! How do you think you will persuade me of that?

S. AUGUSTINE. She has detached your mind from the love of heavenly things and has inclined your heart to love the creature more than the creator: and that path alone leads sooner than any other to death. . . .

PETRARCH. (*He gradually weakens.*) I cannot deny that what you say is true, and I see whither you are step by step leading me.

S. AUGUSTINE. To see it better still, lend me all your attention. Nothing so much leads a man to forget or despise God as the love of things temporal and most of all this passion that we call love. . . .

S. AUGUSTINE. (*The debate continues. Petrarch acknowledges himself beaten.*) One evil is left, to heal you of which I now will make a last endeavor.

PETRARCH. Do so, most gentle father. For though I be not yet wholly set free from my burdens, nonetheless from a great part of them I feel a blessed release.

S. AUGUSTINE. Ambition still has too much hold on you. You seek too eagerly the praise of men and to leave behind you an undying name.

PETRARCH. I freely confess it. I cannot beat down that passion in my soul. For it, as yet, I have found no cure.

S. AUGUSTINE. . . . Now I submit to you that reputation is nothing but talk about some one which many people pass from mouth to mouth.

PETRARCH. I think your definition is a good one.

S. AUGUSTINE. It is then but a breath, a changing wind. And what should disgust you more, it is the breath of a crowd. (*The argument about glory derived from an earthly achievement continues and again poor Petrarch gets the worst of it.*)

PETRARCH. Is it your wish, then, that I should put all my studies aside and renounce every ambition, or would you advise some middle course?

S. AUGUSTINE. I will never advise you to live wholly without ambition, but I would always urge you to put virtue before glory. You know that glory is in a sense the shadow of virtue. And therefore just as it is impossible that your body should not cast a shadow when the sun is shining, so it is impossible also in the light of God Himself that virtues should exist and not cause the glory belonging to them to appear. . . . Here, therefore, is the rule for you to live by: follow after virtue and let glory take care of itself. . . .

And one thing more I beseech you to have in mind: look at the graves of those older than you, but whom nevertheless you have known. Look diligently and then rest assured that the same dwelling-place is also made ready for you. Thither are all of us traveling on. (*The*

*argument ends, as it began, with the solemn facts of
death and the grave.)*

c) Selected Passages from Boccaccio's Decameron.

12. The Black Death of 1348 in Florence. From the
Introduction to *The Decameron*. Bohn's Library.

In the year of our Lord 1348, there happened at
Florence, the finest city in all Italy, a most terrible
plague; which, whether owing to the influence of the
planets, or that it was sent from God as a just punishment for our sins, had broken out some years before in
the Levant, and after passing from place to place and
making incredible havoc all the way, had now reached the
west. There, spite of all the means that art and human
foresight could suggest, such as keeping the city clear
from filth, the exclusion of all suspected persons, and
the publication of copious instructions for the preserva-
tion of health, and notwithstanding manifold humble
supplications offered to God in processions and otherwise, it began to show itself in the spring of the afore-
said year, in a sad and wonderful manner. Unlike what
had been seen in the east, where bleeding from the nose
is the fatal prognostic, here there appeared certain
tumors in the groin or under the arm-pits, some as big
as a small apple, others as an egg; and afterwards purple spots in most parts of the body; in some cases large
and but few in number, in others smaller and more numerous—both sorts the usual messengers of death. To the
cure of this malady neither medical knowledge nor the
power of drugs was of any effect; whether because the
disease was in its own nature mortal, or that the physicians (the number of whom, taking quacks and women

pretenders into the account, was grown very great) could form no just idea of the cause, nor consequently devise a true method of cure; whichever was the reason, few escaped; but nearly all died the third day from the first appearance of the symptoms, some sooner, some later, without any fever or other accessory symptoms. What gave the more virulence to this plague, was that, by being communicated from the sick to the hale, it spread daily, like fire when it comes in contact with large masses of combustibles. Nor was it caught only by conversing with or coming near the sick, but even by touching their clothes, or anything that they had before touched. It is wonderful, what I am going to mention; and had I not seen it with my own eyes, and were there not many witnesses to attest it besides myself, I should never venture to relate it, however worthy it were of belief. Such, I say, was the quality of the pestilential matter, as to pass not only from man to man, but, what is more strange, it has been often known, that anything belonging to the infected, if touched by any other creature, would certainly infect and even kill that creature in a short space of time. One instance of this kind I took particular notice of: the rags of a poor man just dead had been thrown into the street. Two hogs came up, and after rooting amongst the rags and shaking them about in their mouths, in less than an hour they both turned round and died on the spot.

These facts, and others of the like sort, occasioned various fears and devices amongst those who survived, all tending to the same uncharitable and cruel end; which was, to avoid the sick and every thing that had been near them, expecting by that means to save themselves. And some, holding it best to live temperately and to avoid excesses of all kinds, made parties and shut themselves up from the rest of the world; eating and drinking moderately of the best, and diverting themselves with music and such other entertainments as they might have within doors; never listening to anything from without to make them uneasy. Others maintained free living to be a better preservative, and would baulk no passion or appetite they wished to gratify, drinking and revelling incessantly from tavern to tavern, or in private houses (which were frequently found deserted by the owners and therefore common to every one), yet strenuously avoiding, with all this brutal indulgence, to come near the infected.

And such, at that time, was the public distress that the laws, human and divine, were no more regarded; for the officers, to put them in force, being either dead, sick, or in want of persons to assist them, every one did just as he pleased. A third sort of people chose a method between these two: not confining themselves to rules of diet like the former, and yet avoiding the intemperance of the latter; but eating and drinking what their appetites required, they walked everywhere with perfumes and nosegays to smell to, as holding it best to corroborate the brain: for the whole atmosphere seemed to them tainted with the stench of dead bodies, arising partly from the distemper itself, and partly from the fermenting of the medicines within them. Others with less humanity, but perchance, as they supposed, with more security from danger, decided that the only remedy for the pestilence was to avoid it. Persuaded, therefore, of this and taking care for themselves only, men and women in great numbers left the city, their houses, relations, and effects, and fled into the country, as if the wrath of God had been constrained to visit those only within the walls of the

city, or else concluding that none ought to stay in a place
thus doomed to destruction.

13. *The Decameron.* First Day, Novel II. Bohn's Library.

At Paris there lived, as I have been told, a great
merchant and worthy man called Jeannot, a dealer in
silk and an intimate friend to a certain rich Jew, whose
name was Abraham, a merchant also and a very honest
man. Jeannot, being no stranger to Abraham's good and
upright intentions, was greatly troubled that the soul
of so wise and well-meaning a person should perish
through his unbelief. He began, therefore, in the most
friendly manner, to entreat him to renounce the errors
of Judaism and embrace the truth of Christianity, which
he might plainly see flourishing more and more, and as
being the most wise and holy institution, gaining ground,
whereas the religion of the Jews was dwindling to nothing. Abraham answered that he esteemed no religion like
his own; he was born in it and in it he intended to live
and die; nor could anything make him alter his resolu-
tion. All this did not hinder Jeannot from beginning the
same arguments over again in a few days and setting
forth for what reasons our religion ought to be preferred; and though the Jew was well read in his own
law, yet, whether it was his regard for the man or that
Jeannot had the spirit of God upon his tongue, he began
to be greatly pleased with his arguments; but continued
obstinate, nevertheless, in his own creed, and would not
suffer himself to be converted. Jeannot, on the other hand,
was no less persevering in his earnest solicitations, inso-
much that the Jew was overcome by them at last, and

said: "Look you, Jeannot, you are very desirous I should become a Christian and I am so much disposed to do as you would have me, that I intend in the first place to go to Rome, to see him whom you call God's vicar on earth and to consider his ways a little and those of his brother cardinals. If they appear to me in such a light that I may be able to comprehend by them and by what you have said, that your religion is better than mine, as you would persuade me, I will then become a Christian; otherwise I will continue a Jew as I am."

When Jeannot heard this he was much troubled and said to himself: "I have lost all my labor, which I thought well bestowed, expecting to have converted this man; for should he go to Rome and see the wickedness of the clergy there, so far from turning Christian, were he one already, he would certainly again become a Jew." Then addressing Abraham, he said: "Nay, my friend, why should you be at the great trouble and expense of such a journey? Not to mention the dangers, both by sea and land, to which so rich a person as yourself must be exposed, do you think to find nobody here that can baptize you? Or if you have doubt and scruples, where will you meet with abler men than are here to clear them up for you and to answer such questions as you shall put to them?"

"I believe it is as you say," replied the Jew, "but the long and the short of the matter is that I am fully resolved, if you would have me do what you have so much solicited, to go thither, else I will in no wise comply."

Jeannot, seeing him determined, said: "God be with you!" and, supposing that he would never be a Christian after he had seen Rome, gave him over for lost. The Jew took horse and made the best of his way to Rome, where he was most honorably received by his brethren, the Jews; and, without saying a word of what he was come about, he began to look narrowly into the manner of living of the pope, the cardinals, and other prelates, and of the whole court; and from what he himself perceived, being a person of keen observation, and from what he gathered from others, he found that, from the highest to the lowest, they were given to all sorts of lewdness without the least shame or remorse; so that the only way to obtain anything considerable was by applying to prostitutes of every description. He observed, also, that they were generally drunkards and gluttons, and, like brutes, more solicitous about their bellies than anything else. Inquiring further, he found them all such lovers of money that they would not only buy and sell man's blood in general, but even the blood of Christians and sacred things of what kind soever, whether benefices or articles pertaining to the altar. These and other things, which I shall pass over, gave great offense to the Jew, who was a sober and modest person; and now thinking he had seen enough, he returned home.

As soon as Jeannot heard of his arrival he went to see him, thinking of nothing so little as of his conversion. They received one another with a great deal of pleasure and in a day or two, after the traveler had recovered from his fatigue, Jeannot began to inquire of him what he thought of the holy father, the cardinals, and the rest of the court. The Jew immediately answered: "To me it seems as if God was much kinder to them than they deserve; for, if I may be allowed to judge, I must be bold to tell you that I have neither seen sanctity, devotion or anything good in the clergy of Rome; but, on the contrary, luxury, avarice, gluttony, and worse than these, if worse things can be, are so much in fashion with all sorts of people that I should rather esteem the court of Rome to be a forge, if you will allow the expression, for diabolical operations than things divine; and, for all I can perceive, your supreme pastor, and consequently the rest, strive with their whole might and skill to overthrow the Christian religion and to drive it from off the face of the earth, even where they ought to be its chief succor and support. But as I do not see this come to pass which they so earnestly aim at; on the contrary, that your religion gains strength and becomes everyday more glorious, I plainly perceive that it is upheld by the Spirit of God, as the most true and holy of all. For which reason, though I have continued obstinate to your exhortations, now I declare to you that I will no longer defer being made a Christian. Let us go then to the church and do you take care that I be baptized according to the manner of your holy faith."

THE SOURCES

a) Extracts from the Letters of Coluccio Salutati

14. Letter to Giuliano Zonarini, Chancellor of Bologna,
    dated Florence, October 25, 1378. Novati, *Episto-
    lario di Coluccio Salutati,* I, 298 ff.; Emerton, *Hu-
    manism and Tyranny,* p. 290 ff.

. . . And now, my dear colleague, I will come to
a matter in which you have stirred me up in no slight
degree. I wrote to you asking you to buy for me a copy
of Virgil; and you reply reproving me for not occupying
myself with quite different matters and calling Virgil—
to quote your own words—a "lying soothsayer." You
say that, since it is forbidden in the Canon Law to concern oneself with books of that sort, I ought not to
burden you with such an errand; and you generously offer me instead a number of volumes of pious literature.
I beg you, my dearest Giuliano, to pardon me if, in order
that due supremacy of honor be maintained for the prince
of Roman eloquence, the divinest of all poets, Virgil, and
also that I may set you free from the error in which
you seem to be involved, I address you in language rather
more severe than is my wont. . . .

How do you happen, my dear colleague, to have this
dread of Virgil? You say that he records the monstrous

doings of the gods and the vicious practices of men, and that, because he did not, as you say, walk in the way of the Lord, he leads his readers away from the straight path of the faith. . . . Don't imagine that I have ever so read Virgil as to be led to accept his fables about the heathen gods! What I enjoy is his style, hitherto unequalled in verse; nor do I believe it is possible that human talent can ever attain to its loftiness and charm. I admire the majesty of his language, the appropriateness of his words, the harmony of his verses, the elegance of his composition, and the sweetly flowing structure of his sentences.[1]

15. Letter to Giuliano Zonarini, Chancellor of Bologna, dated Florence, May 5, 1379. Novati, *Epistolario di Coluccio Salutati*, I, 321 ff.; Emerton, *Humanism and Tyranny*, p. 301.

(*He again defends Virgil against the contention that serious-minded Christians should not occupy themselves with the pagan authors, but cautiously takes a middle ground.*)

I would not deny, seeing that we live in a world of transient things, that it is better to reach heaven by the straight way, through the study of the sacred writings than through the twistings and turnings of the poets (*that is, the pagan writers in general and Virgil in particular*). But, in view of the fact that both roads properly followed lead to the same desired goal, though the former is to be preferred, the latter should not be neglected.

---

[1] This and the following selections from *Humanism and Tyranny* by Ephraim Emerton used by the courtesy of the Harvard University Press.

16. Letter to Brother John of San Miniato, dated Florence, January 25, 1406. Novati, IV, pt. 1, 170; Emerton, *Humanism and Tyranny*, p. 312 ff.

I read recently, Venerable Father in Christ, the letter which you wrote to that very dear son of mine, Angelo Corbellini, and was greatly amused by it. You are trying, according to your habit, to draw him away from poetry and secular studies; or, to put it more exactly, to frighten him away from them. Whether you are right in so doing is your affair, and I leave you to the reproaches of my distinguished friend, John of Ravenna, and the many others who hold contrary opinions (*that is, the whole body of the humanists*). . . .

What right have you, I beg you, to forbid my friend Angelo to indulge his taste for oratory, poetry, and philosophy? What rights have you over any one outside your monastery? True, it is right for you and for every one to encourage and even command that which is honorable and to prohibit the contrary, but what is there in these things which makes it right to forbid them? I know and read daily in St. Jerome, St. Ambrose, and St. Augustine splendid passages from the philosophers and orators and verses from the poets which shine out like stars from those most sacred writings; and I do not suppose you condemn this in them as a crime. If things true and holy, decorous and beautiful, are found in those doctors of the Church and may be read there without harm, why should these same things be called profane and infamous in the original writings of their authors? Why are they forbidden to us if they were permitted to holy doctors?

17. Letter to Brother John Dominici of the Dominican Order, dated Florence, 1406. Novati IV, pt. 1, 205 ff.; Emerton, *Humanism and Tyranny,* p. 346 ff.

(*This letter, or rather treatise, begun in the last year of his life, Salutati did not live to finish. It is the most elaborate defense of humanistic studies against monkish obscurantists he ever made.*) I will then, Reverend Father, begin with you a discussion as to whether it is more satisfactory and convenient to commence our education with sacred literature or to spend some time on profane studies. (*He then takes up the subjects of the trivium—grammar, dialectic, rhetoric—which revolve around the Latin language and literature, and shows that they are absolutely necessary for the comprehension and defense of Christian doctrine. Note again that if he breaks a lance for humanism, he does so on the understanding that humanism, properly pursued, strengthens and does not undermine the faith. Having justified the trivium, he turns to the quadrivium, composed of arithmetic, geometry, music, and astronomy and embracing whatever there was of science in the medieval curriculum. A few passages will serve to illustrate his attitude, which, though untouched by science in a modern sense, is free from superstition in its grosser forms.*) I do not think that anything can be found in these branches of learning which contradicts our beliefs. Even though some among those accepted as established truths not to be questioned by human intelligence were shown to be false, still this would have nothing to do with the faith and would not contradict any doctrine that is true. . . . What can I say of astronomy, which, as we view the heavenly bodies with their varied movements, the vastness of the universe, the glory of the earth and sky, directs the creature to the creator of all things? And in this what can be found contrary to Holy Scripture? True, I agree with St. Augustine that prophecies of the future, such as the astrologers put forth, are absolute nonsense. I do not think that such foolishness should be reckoned among the Liberal Arts, whatever others may think.

THE SOURCES

Part III. Strengthening of the New Interests; Weakening of the Old Interests

a) Leonardo Bruni Extols the Greek Language and Literature

18. Extract from Bruni's History of his own Times in Italy (*Commentarius rerum suo tempore in Italia gestarum*). Muratori, *Scriptores,* vol. 19, p. 920.

Then first came the knowledge of Greek letters, which for seven hundred years had been lost among us. It was the Byzantine, Chrysoloras, a nobleman in his own country and most skilled in literature, who brought Greek learning back to us. Because his country was invaded by the Turks, he came by sea to Venice; but as soon as his fame went abroad, he was cordially invited and eagerly besought to come to Florence on a public salary to spread his abundant riches before the youth of the city (*This took place in 1396*). At that time I was studying Civil Law. But my nature was afire with the love of learning and I had already given no little time to dialectic and rhetoric. Therefore at the coming of Chrysoloras I was divided in my mind, feeling that it was a shame to desert the Law and no less wrong to let slip such an occasion for learning Greek. And often with youthful impulsiveness I addressed myself thus: "When you are privileged to gaze upon and have converse with Homer, Plato, and Demosthenes as well as the other poets, philosophers, and orators of whom such wonderful things are reported, and when you might saturate yourself with their admirable teachings, will you turn your back and flee? Will you permit this opportunity, divinely offered you, to slip by? For seven hundred years now no one in Italy has been in possession of Greek and yet we agree that all knowledge comes from that source. What great advancement of knowledge, enlargement of fame, and increase of pleasure will come to you from an acquaintance with this tongue! There are everywhere quantities of doctors of the Civil Law and the opportunity of completing your study in this field will not fail you. However, should the one and only doctor of Greek letters disappear, there will be no one from whom to acquire them."

Overcome at last by these arguments, I gave myself to Chrysoloras and developed such ardor that whatever I learned by day, I revolved with myself in the night while asleep. I had many fellow-students, two of the number who were particularly proficient belonging to the Florentine nobility. . . . A little later came Pietro Vergerio (*the celebrated writer on education quoted in Section IV*).

b) *Selections from Poygio's "Facetiae" and Letters*

19. Concerning a Priest Who Buried a Pet Dog. A story from the *Facetiae* or Jocose Tales of Poggio, I, p. 65 f.

There lived in Tuscany a well-to-do priest. Having lost a little dog of which he was very fond, he buried him in the churchyard (*i. e., in consecrated ground re-*

served for Christians). This came to the ears of the bishop, who, coveting the priest's money, summoned him for punishment as if he had committed a great crime. The parish priest, who had a shrewd understanding of his bishop, answered the summons and came provided with fifty golden ducats. The prelate reproached him sternly for the burial of the dog and ordered him to prison. "O father," replied the cunning priest, "if you only knew the wisdom of that little animal, you would not wonder that he deserved burial along with human beings. For his intelligence was human in his lifetime and more than human when he came to die." "What do you mean by that?" asked the bishop. "At the end of his days," the priest rejoined, "he made his will and, knowing that you are a poor man, he left you the fifty ducats which I have here in my hand." Thereupon the bishop approved the burial, pocketed the money, and bade the priest depart in peace.

20. Letter from Poggio to Leonardo Bruni, dated Constance, 1416. O. Gratius, *Fasciculus rerum* etc., p. 304 ff.

When I returned to Constance (*where the great Council of the Church was in session*), the case of Jerome of Prague was taken up, whom they openly call a heretic. I have resolved to recount the case to you because of its importance and, even more, because of the eloquence and learning of the man. I confess that I have never seen any one, who, in defending a case involving the sentence of death, came nearer to the persuasiveness of the ancients, whom we so greatly admire. Wonderful it was to witness the eloquence, the arguments, the bearing, and the confidence with which he confronted his adversaries and

brought his plea to an end. So that one must needs grieve
that a spirit so noble and lofty should have been lured
into the paths of heresy, if indeed those things which
are charged against him are true. Not that it is my affair
to judge a matter of this sort. I accept the opinion of
those who are considered wiser than I. Nor shall I give
a detailed report of the case after the manner of the
rhetoricians. That would be tedious and take many days.
I shall touch only upon the high places, from which you
will be able to gather the learning of the man.

Although many things had been brought against this
Jerome which seemed to indicate that he was a heretic,
and although these were confirmed by the testimony of
witnesses, the Council decided that he should reply publicly and serially to all the charges which had been
brought against him. When, on being led into the assembly, he was ordered to reply to the bill of particulars,
he refused, saying that he ought to be allowed to state
his own case rather than to meet the slanders of his adversaries. Later he would then take up the calumnies
which his adversaries had directed against him. But when
this request was refused, standing in the midst of the
assembly, he said: "How great a wrong is this, that
while for three hundred and forty days I have suffered
the most cruel confinement, in squalor and filth, in want
of everything, you constantly gave audience to my opponents and detractors, and now refuse to hear me one
single hour! Thus it follows that, while the ears of all
of you have been open to these whispers and you have
been persuaded through constant repetition that I am a
heretic, an enemy of the faith, a persecutor of the clergy,
yet to me no opportunity is given for defending myself.
If you have judged me beforehand in your minds to be
a dishonest man, how will you be able to determine

what I really am? You are men, not gods; not immortal, but mortal; you are able to err, to be deceived, and led astray. In this Council are said to be the lights of the world, the wisest men alive. The rather does it behoove you to see to it that nothing be done unadvisedly or against justice. As for me, I am a man whose head is at stake. And yet I say these things not for my own sake, a poor mortal, but because it seems unworthy of your wisdom to arraign against me so many men in violation of all justice and because the example here set will prove injurious." These and many things beside he said most appropriately, often interrupted by the noise and murmurs of the audience.

Then it was decreed that he should first answer to the errors which were charged against him and that afterwards he should be permitted to say what he pleased. Thereupon the heads of the accusation were read one by one from the pulpit and supported with testimony. This done, he was asked if he had aught to object. Unbelievable it is how hotly he rejoined and with what arguments he defended himself. . , .

When on account of the number and weight of the charges it was impossible to complete the case on this day, it was continued to a third day when the heads of the various accusations were repeated and substantiated by many witnesses. Thereupon rising, he said: "Since you have listened so attentively to my opponents, it is right and proper that you should hear me with open minds." At length, in spite of noisy objections, permission was given him to speak. To begin with, he prayed that God should grant him the necessary ability and illumination to turn the occasion to the profit and salvation of his soul. "I know, most reverend doctors," he said thereupon, "that many excellent men, bearing up bravely against indignities and overwhelmed with false witnesses, have been condemned with iniquitous judgments." And at the very start he referred to Socrates, who, when unjustly condemned by his fellow-citizens, was yet unwilling to seize the opportunity to escape. Then he mentioned the captivity of Plato, the flight of Anaxagoras, the torture of Zeno, and the unjust condemnation of many other pagans. Thence he passed to Hebrew examples, and first instanced Moses, the liberator and legislator of his people. Often had he been calumniated by his people and called the betrayer and the despiser of his race. Coming down to John the Baptist and to our Savior, he proceeded to show how they were condemned by false witnesses and false judges.

He declared that it was a crime that a priest should be unjustly condemned by a priest and the greatest crime of all that this should be done by a company of priests. . . . He unfolded his life and studies and how he had striven to serve and be virtuous. It was formerly the custom of the most learned and holy of men that they held different opinions in matters of faith, not to the injury of the faith but to the discovery of the truth. In this way Augustine and Jerome disagreed, holding not only different opinions, but even contrary ones—and this with no suspicion of heresy. So coming down to John Huss, who had died at the stake (*in the previous year*), he called him a good, just, and holy man, who did not deserve such a death. And he added that he himself was prepared to go to any punishment whatsoever with brave and steadfast mind. In praise of John Huss he declared that Huss had never said anything in criticism of the Church of God, but only against the abuses of the clergy, against the pride, pomp, and display of prelates. For since the wealth of the Church was intended first for the poor, secondly for the hospitals, and thirdly for the building of churches, it seemed to this good man a disgrace that it should be wasted upon harlots, banquets, food for horses and dogs, vestments, and other things unworthy of the religion of Christ. . . .

For three hundred and forty days he lay in the pit of a foul, dark tower. He complained of the severity of this treatment, asserting that, as became a good and brave man, he did not complain because he had to bear these indignities, but because he marveled at the inhumanity shown him. In the dungeon, far from reading, he could not even see. . . .

He stood there fearless and intrepid, not alone despising death but seeking it, as though he were another Cato. O, man worthy to be remembered forever! I praise not that which he advanced, if anything, against the institutions of the Church. But I admire his learning, his wide knowledge, his eloquence, his suavity, his pregnant answers. But I fear that nature has given all these things to him only for his destruction. A period of two days was allotted him for repentance. Many of the most learned men approached him in the hope of persuading him to retract. But when with increasing obstinacy he clung to his errors and was condemned by the Council as a heretic and burned with fire, he went to his fate with joyful and uplifted countenance. For he feared not the fire nor suffering nor death.

c) *Aeneas Silvius Piccolomini (afterwards Pope Pius II)*
describes Genoa.

21. Letter to Andreozo Petrucci in Siena, dated Milan, March 24, 1432. *Der Briefwechsel des E. S. Piccolomini, herausgegeben von R. Wolkan. Fontes*

Rerum Austriacarum. II Abtheilung. Band LXI, p. 7.

Would you were with me! You would see a city which has no equal anywhere on earth. It lies upon a hill over which rude mountains tower, while the lower city is washed by the waves of the sea. The harbor is bow-shaped so that storms can not do the ships any harm. . . . It constitutes thus a thoroughly reliable anchorage sought by ships big as hills, triremes and countless other craft. And what a coming and going there is! From the east they hail and from the west, so that you may see daily people of the most different sort with unimaginable rough manners and customs and traders with every conceivable ware. Right at the shore arise the most magnificent palaces, heaven-scaling, built of marble, decorated with columns and often too with sculptures. Under them runs an arcade for the length of a thousand steps where every conceivable object is for sale. The rest of the city winds upward along the side of the hill. In this section the houses are so large and distinguished that a king or a prince might be content with any one of them. For they are all of royal magnificence, though they stand closely together and the streets are narrow to the point of permitting only two or three people to pass abreast. The churches, beautiful as they are, do not seem to me to be worthy of such a city. However, they are not without splendor and boast more particularly some handsome sepulchral monuments in honor of deceased noblemen. Certain relics enjoy considerable veneration. I examined the emerald bowl, from which, according to the legend, our Savior ate with his disciples, and found it marvelously luminous. The city is notably well supplied with water from mountain sources which is distributed to the individual houses and is of especial excellence of taste.

Now as to the life and customs of the population. The men are substantial, well-grown, and impressive, carry themselves proudly and are in fact proud. They are a gifted folk, not likely to be found inferior to any other people in the quality of their mind. Strenuous labors, night-watches, and self-denials they bear easily. Their deeds of bravery at sea are incredible; incredible too the perils they confront and the difficulties they master. Our helmsman, a certain Ottobono Imperiali, who has been living at sea now for twenty-three years, has never slept between walls, and never, as he told us, did he change his clothes, even when he was drenched with water. The advantages that come with profits and riches offer compensation for past hardships. In case of a war at sea one does well to take their experience and skill into account, for victory depends solely on them. Should they desire it, victory is certain; should they be contrary-minded, there is no prospect of success since they are the lords of the sea and every one trembles before them.

They dress nobly and elegantly. As for their women, they let them do as they please, for rather may it be said that the women wield the scepter than the other way about. They are not afflicted with thirst for education, though they learn languages as they need them. For other elements of the Liberal Arts they have little use, except as a possible relief from business. Every man selects a woman to whom he pays court. A strange thing is that they maintain irregular relations with other men's wives and at the same time are not in the least offended with the carryings-on of their own wives. Thus it happens that the women of this city enjoy great freedom; indeed it would not be an exaggeration to designate Genoa as the paradise of women. . . . Their dresses are luxurious, loaded with gold and silver trimmings and with jewels. On their fingers sparkle emeralds and diamonds supplied by India and Persia. For where it is a question of adornment they fear no expense. They bother neither about the household nor about needle and dishes, for every house enjoys abundant service. I remember a woman who was not even a woman of rank—when her son-in-law asked her what she had prepared for his breakfast, she made answer that she had not been in the kitchen for seven years. These women are all very easy-going, refuse to make an effort, and do not wait for the holidays to enjoy themselves with their admirers. They are always showing themselves in their best clothes. Indeed the more I reflect upon this city, the more I am convinced that Venus in our time no longer dwells in Cyprus or on Cytheron but in this city of Genoa. Here seems to me to be her shrine. . . .

Even the nuns are not held to a rigorous standard. They go about at pleasure whither they will. It is incredible that this should not distract them from their purpose. Nor do they, as is said to be the case with us (*i. e., the Sienese*), curse their parents who confined them in the cloister. They are very numerous and much more merry than the married women, evidently because they do not bear the yoke of matrimony.

d) Lorenzo Valla Proves the So-called Donation of Constantine to be a Forgery

22. Extracts from the *Treatise of Lorenzo Valla on the Donation of Constantine*. Text and Translation into English by Christopher B. Coleman.

(*The so-called Donation of Constantine purported to*

record the gift of the western half of the Roman Empire by the first Christian emperor, Constantine the Great, to Pope Sylvester (314–336 A. D.). The document, forged a little past the middle of the eighth century in the interest of the territorial aspirations of the papacy, was accepted as genuine till the fifteenth century and played a large part in the claim of the medieval popes to temporal supremacy over the sovereigns of Europe. Valla was not the first scholar to doubt its genuineness, but he was the first to demolish it utterly and publicly. When launching his attack in 1440, he was secretary to the King of Naples and pursued as his immediate end the undermining of the papal claim to suzerainty over his master.)

. . . I know that for a long time now men's ears are waiting to hear the offense with which I charge the Roman pontiffs. It is indeed an enormous one, due either to supine ignorance, or to gross avarice, . . . or to the pride of empire. For during some centuries now either they have not known that the Donation of Constantine is spurious and forged or else they themselves forged it; and their successors, walking in the same way of deceit as their elders, have defended as true what they knew to be false, dishonoring the majesty of the pontificate, the memory of ancient pontiffs, and the Christian religion. . . . The popes say the city of Rome is theirs, theirs the kingdom of Sicily and of Naples, the whole of Italy, the Gauls, the Spains, the Germans, the Britons, indeed the whole West. For all these are contained in the instrument of the Donation itself.

So all these are yours, supreme pontiff? And it is your purpose to recover them all? To despoil all kings and princes of the West of their cities or compel them to pay you a yearly tribute? Is that your plan? I, on the contrary, think it fairer to let the princes despoil you of all the empire you hold. For, as I shall show, that Donation whence the supreme pontiffs derive their right was known neither to Pope Sylvester nor to Emperor Constantine.

(*After discussing the inherent improbability of the surrender of the West by the emperor to the pope, he reviews the contemporary evidence and shows that it all tends to prove that the emperors, beginning with Constantine himself, continued to exercise rule over the West and that the popes did not exercise it.*)

Come now, was Pope Sylvester ever in possession? Who dispossessed him? For he did not have possession permanently nor did any of his successors, at least till Gregory the Great (*590–604 A. D.*), and there is nothing to prove that Gregory had possession. One that is not in possession and can not prove that he has been dispossessed, certainly never did have possession; and if he says he did, he is mad. You see, I even prove that you are mad! Or if you be not, tell me who dislodged Sylvester? Did Constantine himself do it, or his sons, or Julian, or some other Caesar? Give the name of the expeller, give the date. From what place was the pope expelled first, whence next, and so in order? . . . Did he lose everything in a single day or gradually and by districts? . . .

(*He takes up the document in detail to show its historical and philological absurdities. The first paragraph he reviews contains a passage, according to which the emperor, "together with all our satraps and the whole senate and nobles also," declares it to be proper to endow the pope with every power and dignity because he represented God on earth.*)

O thou scoundrel, thou villain (*i. e., the forger*)! The Life of Sylvester (*a genuine document, let it be noted*), which you allege as your evidence, says that for a long time no one of senatorial rank was willing to accept the Christian religion and that Constantine was obliged to solicit the Roman poor with bribes to be baptized. And you venture to say that, within the first days, the senate, the nobles, the satraps, as though already Christians, together with the emperor passed decrees for the honoring of the Roman Church! What have satraps got to do with the case? Numskull, blockhead! Do emperors speak thus? Are Roman decrees drafted thus? Whoever heard of satraps in any Roman province?

(*The forger makes the blunder of speaking of Constantinople as a patriarchate of the Church.*)

How in the world . . . could one speak of Constantinople as one of the patriarchal sees, when it was not yet a patriarchate, nor a see, nor a Christian city, nor named Constantinople, nor founded, nor planned! For the concession was granted, so the document says, the third day after Emperor Constantine became a Christian. And at that time Byzantium, not Constantinople, occupied that site. . . .

(*Having demolished the document with his critical acumen, Valla declares that the popes, under the Donation, have become evil stewards.*)

Wherefore I declare and cry aloud . . . that in my time no one in the supreme pontificate has been either a faithful or prudent steward, but they have been so far from giving food to the household of God that they have devoured their income as food and a mere morsel of bread! The pope himself makes war on peaceable people and sows discord among states and princes. The pope both thirsts for the goods of others and drinks up his own. . . . Not only does he enrich himself at the expense of the empire . . . but he enriches himself at the expense of even the Church and the Holy Spirit. . . . And when he is reminded of this by good people occasionally, he does not deny it but openly admits it and boasts that he is free to wrest from its occupants by any means whatever the patrimony given to the Church by Constantine. . . .

And so that he may recover the missing parts of the Donation, he spends money wickedly stolen from good people and supports armed forces, mounted and on foot, while Christ is dying of hunger in many thousands of paupers. Nor does he know, the unworthy reprobate, that while he works to deprive secular powers of what belongs to them, they in turn are either led by his bad example or driven by necessity . . . to make off with what belongs to the Church. And so there is no religion anywhere, no sanctity, no fear of God. And, what I shudder to mention, impious men pretend to find in the pope an excuse for all their crimes . . .

If only I may see the time when the pope is the vicar of Christ alone and not of Caesar also! . . . Then the pope will be the Holy Father in fact as well as in name, Father of all, Father of the Church; nor will he stir up wars among Christians but those stirred up by others he, through his apostolic powers and papal majesty, will bring to an end.[1]

e) Selections from the "Vite" (Lives) of Vespasiano

23. Selections from the Life of Pope Nicholas V (1447–1455). *Vite di Uomini Illustri del Secolo XV* by de Vespasiano da Bisticci, p. 20 ff.

[1] This selection from *The Treatise of Lorenzo Valla on the Donation of Constantine* by Christopher B. Coleman is used by courtesy of the Yale University Press.

At this time came the year of jubilee (1450), and since it was a true jubilee, coming, according to the law of the Church, at the end of a period of fifty years, the concourse of people at Rome was such that a greater had never been known. It was a wonderful thing to see the great masses of folk. In Rome and Florence the streets were so crowded that the people seemed like swarms of ants; and at the bridge of Sant' Angelo (*in Rome*) there was such a crowd of people of every sort and condition that they were jammed together and unable to move in any direction. In the struggles that ensued between those who came to seek indulgences and those who were already gathered at the place, more than two hundred persons, male and female, lost their lives. When Pope Nicholas a man of great compassion, heard of the accident, he was greatly displeased and made provision to prevent a recurrence. He also ordered to be built at the approach to the bridge two small churches in memory of the destruction of so many men upon the occasion of the jubilee; and he took charge of their burial.

Much money came by this means to the Apostolic See. With this the pope began to erect buildings in many places; and he sent for Greek and Latin books, wherever he was able to find them without regard to price. He gathered together a large company of writers, the worthiest he could find, and kept them in steady employment. He also summoned a number of learned men, both to compose new works and to translate such works as were not already translated, giving them most abundant advances for their needs. And when the works were ready and brought to him he gave the writers additional sums of money in order that they should more willingly labor in his behalf. . . . He gathered together collections of

books upon every subject, both Greek and Latin, to the
number of 5000 volumes. At his death it was found by
inventory that never since the time of Ptolemy had half
so large a number of books of every kind been brought
together. Any book he heard of he caused to be copied
without regard to what it cost him; and few were the
places where his Holiness had not copiers at work. . . .

It was Pope Nicholas' intention to found a library in
St. Peter's for the common use of the whole Roman
court. And this would have been an admirable thing indeed if he had been able to carry it out; but death pre-
vented his bringing it to completion. He threw light
upon the Holy Scriptures with innumerable books which
he caused to be translated; and the same may be said
of the classics, including certain works upon grammar,
useful for learning Latin. Among these was the *Orthog-
raphy* of Messer Giovanni Tortello, who was of his
Holiness's household and presided over the library. This
book of his is held in high esteem by grammarians. Then
there was the *Iliad* of Homer and Strabo's *De situ orbis*
which latter he caused to be translated by Guarino. And
he gave him 500 florins for each part, that is, for Asia,
Africa, and Europe, making in all 1500 florins. Herodo-
tus and Thucydides he had translated by Messer Lorenzo
Valla and rewarded him liberally for his trouble. Xenophon and Diodorus he assigned to Messer Poggio; Poly-
bius to Nicolo Perotto. And when the latter handed him
the work, he gave him 300 fresh-minted papal ducats in
a purse, saying at the same time that it was not what the
writer deserved, but that in time he would take care to
satisfy him. (*There follows a long list of additional
authors, classical and patristic.*) Many other works were
translated and composed at the desire of his Holiness,

of which I have no knowledge. I have mentioned only those of which I know.

24. Selections from the Life of Cosimo de' Medici (1389-1464). *Vite di Uomini Illustri,* p. 246 ff.

When Cosimo had finished the residence and a large part of the church (*La Badia*), he began to reflect how he might have the place peopled with goodly men of letters; and presently he hit upon the plan of founding a fine library. One day when I happened to be with him in his room, he said to me: "How would you go about this library?" I replied that as for buying the books it would be impossible, for they were not to be had. Thereupon he said: "How can it be done?" When I told him that it would be necessary to have the books copied, he asked if I would be willing to undertake the task. I answered that I was. Then he told me to set about the work and that he would leave everything to me; and as for the money that would be necessary, he would refer the matter to Don Arcangelo, the prior of the monastery, who would draw bills upon the bank which should be paid. The library was begun at once, for it was his will that no time should be lost. And as I was given all the money I needed, I assembled quickly forty-five writers and finished two hundred volumes in twenty-two months. We made use of the excellent plan of the library of Pope Nicholas, which the pope communicated to Cosimo in the form of a catalogue made out by his own hand.

As for the contents of the library, in the first place there are the Bible and the Concordances with all their commentaries, ancient and modern. And the first writer who commented on the Holy Scriptures and showed the manner of commenting to all the others was Origen. He wrote in Greek and St. Jerome translated that part of his work which deals with the five books of Moses. Then there are the works of St. Ignatius the martyr, who wrote in Greek and was a disciple of St. John the evangelist; most fervent in his Christian zeal, he wrote and preached and by his labors won the crown of martyrdom. Further, there are the works of St. Basil, bishop of Cappadocia, a Greek; those of St. Gregory of Nazianzen, of Gregory of Nyssa, his brother, of St. John Chrysostom, of St. Athanasius of Alexandria, of St. Ephrem the Monk, of John Climacus, also a Greek. All the works of the Greek doctors which have been translated into Latin are there. Then follow the holy doctors and writers in Latin, beginning with the works of Lactantius, who was very ancient and had worthy qualities; Hilary of Poitou, a most grave doctor; St. Cyprian of Carthage, most elegant and saintly; the works of Tertullian, a very learned Carthaginian. Further, the four doctors of the Latin Church are represented by all their works; and no other library has these works complete. Next come the works of St. Jerome, all the works of St. Gregory, the moral doctor, all the works of St. Bernard the Abbott as well as those of Hugh of St. Victor, of St. Anselm, of St. Isidore of Seville, of Bede, of Rabanus Maurus. On coming to the modern doctors we note St. Thomas Aquinas, Albert the Great, Alexander of Hales, St. Bonaventure, the Archbishop Antonino of Florence, more particularly his *Summa*.

Turning to the philosophers, we list of the works of Aristotle both his Moral and Natural Philosophy; all the commentaries of St. Thomas and Albert the Great as well as of others on the philosophy of Aristotle; Aristotle's Logic and other modern systems of logic. In Canon Law, there are the *Decretum,* the Decretals, *Liber Sex-*

tus, the Clementines, the *Summa* of the bishop of Ostia;
Innocent; the lectures of the bishop of Ostia on the Decretals; Giovanni Andrea on *Liber Sextus;* an anonymous
lecture on the *Decretum;* and still other works on Canon
Law by the abbott of Cicilia and others. Of histories
there will be found all the Ten Books of Livy, Caesar's
Commentaries, Suetonius Tranquillus on the Lives of the
Emperors, Plutarch's Lives, Quintus Curtius on the
Deeds of Alexander the Great, Sallust on *De bello Jugur-
thino et Catilinario.* (*And many more titles which are
here omitted.*) The Library contains also all the works
of Tully in three volumes; all the works of Seneca in one
volume; Quintilian, *De institutione oratoria* and the Dec-
lamations. . . . Of poets the following are represented:
Virgil, Terence, Ovid, Lucan, Statius, Seneca, Plautus;
and of grammarians, Priscian. And all the other works
necessary to a library were there, not one being missing.
And since there were not copies of all these works in
Florence, we sent to Milan, to Bologna, and to other
places, wherever they might be found. Cosimo lived to
see the library completed as well as the cataloguing and
the arranging of the books. In all of which he took great
pleasure, everything being done, as was his custom, with
great promptness.

THE SOURCES

PART IV. THE NEW EDUCATION

The following four treatises on education startlingly reveal how far the new mental outlook had gone toward reconstructing the theory and practice of education. While the new classical learning plays a large part in the curriculum, instruction in hygiene, games, and practical ethics is not neglected because the end kept constantly in view is the preparation of youth for the actual struggle of life. And Christianity, let it be observed, remains the kernel of instruction, even though it seems at times to disappear from view behind the proud parade of pagan poets, philosophers, and historians. Without question the ideal aimed at by this education is not, as is sometimes charged, the literary trifler and religious sceptic, but the well-rounded, active Christian gentleman. Moreover, education is not for all but is the prerogative and ornament of an upper class.

All four of the treatises are cast in the form of letters. That of Vergerio was composed, probably in 1404, for the use of the son of the lord of Padua. Piccolomini wrote his tract, also for a young prince, the king of Hungary, in 1450. Bruni's essay is remarkable in that it was addressed, around 1405, to a studious young woman of the Montefeltro family. It is interesting that in the opinion of the writer a woman might aspire to much the same education as a man. Guarino's treatise, written in 1459, may be taken to describe the actual system of instruction followed in his father's famous school at Ferrara. As a practicing school-master's statement, it is more definite and narrow than the others.

Not for many generations did the theory and practice of education in Europe and America advance beyond the stage described in these documents. In fact it was not till the nineteenth century that the humanistic curriculum was gradually revised in the interest of studies, such as science, which had been for some time coming to the front. And not till the last score or so of years may the humanistic program be said to have disappeared entirely before the new and revolutionary curriculum devised with strict regard to the altered needs of our twentieth century society. But if our present educational *practice* no longer squares with that of these pamphlets, it is noteworthy that our *theory,* involving the general principles which should serve as our guide in preparing young men and women for work and service in the world, has not advanced far beyond the position defined in these documents. Such a statement pays a merited tribute to the universal and noble inspiration of these educators who stand at the threshold of the Modern Age.

25. Selections from Pietro Paolo Vergerio's *De Ingenuis Moribus.* Woodward, *Vittorino da Feltre and other Humanist Educators,* p. 96 ff.

We call those studies *liberal* which are worthy of a free man; those studies by which we attain and practise virtue and wisdom; that education which calls forth, trains and develops those highest gifts of body and of mind which ennoble men, and which are rightly judged to rank next in dignity to virtue only. For to a vulgar temper gain and pleasure are the one aim of existence; to a lofty nature, moral worth and fame. It is, then, of the highest importance that even from infancy this aim, this effort, should constantly be kept alive in growing minds. For I may affirm with fullest conviction that we shall not have attained wisdom in our later years unless in our earliest we have sincerely entered on its search.

. . . .

How many are the gaps which the ignorance of past ages has wilfully caused in the long and noble roll of writers! Books—in part or in their entirety—have been allowed to perish. What remains of others is often sorely corrupt, mutilated or imperfect. It is hard that no slight portion of the history of Rome is only to be known through the labors of an author writing in the Greek language (*Pultarch*); it is still worse that this same noble tongue, once well nigh the daily speech of our race, as familiar as the Latin language itself, is on the point of perishing even amongst its own sons, and to us Italians is already utterly lost, unless we except one or two who in our time are tardily endeavouring to rescue something —if it be only a mere echo of it—from oblivion (*Vergerio was among these rescuers of Greek*).

We come now to the consideration of the various subjects which may rightly be included under the name of "Liberal Sudies." Amongst these I accord the first place to history, on grounds both of its attractiveness and of its utility, qualities which appeal equally to the scholar and to the statesman. Next in importance ranks moral philosophy, which indeed is, in a peculiar sense, a Liberal Art, in that its purpose is to teach men the secret of true freedom. History, then, gives us the concrete examples of the precepts inculcated by philosophy. The one shows what men should do, the other what men have said and done in the past and what practical lessons we may draw therefrom for the present day. I would indicate as the third main branch of study, eloquence, which indeed holds a place of distinction amongst the refined arts. By philosophy we learn the essential truth of things, which by eloquence we so exhibit in orderly adornment as to bring conviction to differing minds. And history provides the light of experience—a cumulative wisdom fit to supplement the force of reason and the persuasion of eloquence. For we allow that soundness of judgment, wisdom of speech, integrity of conduct are the marks of a truly liberal temper.

. . . .

The Art of Letters rests upon a different footing. It is a study adapted to all times and to all circumstances, to the investigation of fresh knowledge or to the recasting and application of old. Hence the importance of grammar and of the rules of composition must be recognized at the outset, as the foundation on which the whole study of literature must rest: and closely associated with these rudiments, the art of disputation or logical argument. The function of this is to enable us to discern fallacy from truth in discussion. Logic, indeed, as setting forth the true method of learning, is the guide to the acquisition of knowledge in whatever subject. Rhetoric comes next, and is strictly speaking the formal study by which we attain the art of eloquence; which, as we have just stated, takes the third place amongst the studies specially important in public life.

. . . .

As to music, the Greeks refused the title of 'educated' to anyone who could not sing or play. Socrates set an example to the Athenian youth by himself learning to play in his old age; urging the pursuit of music not as a sensuous indulgence, but as an aid to the inner harmony of the soul. In so far as it is taught as a healthy recreation for the moral and spiritual nature, music is a truly Liberal Art, and, both as regards its theory and its practice, should find a place in education.

Arithmetic, which treats of the properties of numbers, geometry, which treats of the properties of dimensions, lines, surfaces, and solid bodies, are weighty studies because they possess a peculiar element of certainty. The science of the stars, their motions, magnitudes and distances, lifts us into the clear calm of the upper air. There we may contemplate the fixed stars, or the conjunctions of the planets, and predict the eclipses of the sun and the moon. The knowledge of nature, animate and inanimate, the laws and the properties of things in heaven and in earth, their causes, mutations and effects, especially the explanation of their wonders (as they are popularly supposed) by the unravelling of their causes—this is a most delightful, and at the same time a most profitable, study for youth. With these may be joined investigations concerning the weights of bodies and those relative to the subject which mathematicians call "perspective."

I may here glance for a moment at the three great professional disciplines: medicine, law, theology. Medicine, which is applied science, has undoubtedly much that makes it attractive to a student. But it cannot be described as a liberal study. Law, which is based upon moral philosophy, is undoubtedly held in high respect. Regarding law as a subject of study, such respect is entirely deserved; but law as practised becomes a mere trade. Theology, on the other hand, treats of themes removed from our senses and attainable only by pure intelligence.

. . . .

It is of greatest importance that boys should be trained

from childhood in feats of courage and endurance. The Lacedaemonian discipline was indeed severe. The boys were trained to be of such temper that in their contests they would not yield nor confess themselves vanquished; the severest tests produced no cry of pain, though blood might flow and consciousness itself give way. The result was that all antiquity rehearses the deathless courage of the Spartans in the field. Their arms were to them part of their very selves, to be cast away, or laid down, only with their lives. What else than this same early and most diligent training could have enabled the Romans to show themselves so valiant, so enduring, in the campaigns they fought? Wherefore, whether a boy be trained in arms or in letters (for these are the two chief Liberal Arts and fittest therefore for a prince), so soon as he be able to use his limbs let him be trained to arms; so soon as he can rightly speak let him be trained to letters. Further, it will be easy and it will be of great benefit to a boy to alternate the study of letters with bodily exercises. And, indeed, at whatever age he may be, the same practice is to be commended. The Emperor Theodosius, we are told, spent the day in martial exercises or in the business of the state; the evening he devoted to books.

In choice of bodily exercises those should be adopted which serve to maintain the body in good health and to strengthen the limbs. And thus it will be necessary to consider to some extent the case of each individual boy.

. . . .

But as we are not so constituted that we are able to bestow ourselves all day long upon our ordered tasks, I will now set forth the true place of recreation. First of all, it imports that boys engage in no debasing games or such as cannot develop bodily gifts or powers of will. We cannot, therefore, accord a high place to that practice which found favor with Scipio and Laelius, namely, of seeking rest for exhausted minds in aimless walks along the shore, picking up pebbles and shells as they went. Scaevola, on the other hand, was wiser: having spent wearisome days in the courts, he found in the sharp exertion of ball-play the best refreshment alike for jaded spirits and for bodily fatigue. So, too, others seek recreation in hunting, hawking, or fishing; and so keen is their enjoyment that the severe efforts which these pursuits demand are cheerfully borne.

"The labour we delight in physicks pain."

. . . .

Lastly, I must add a word upon attention to personal habits. In this matter we must not be neglectful for, whilst we should not bestow too much thought upon our outward appearance, which is effeminacy, we must have due regard to our dress and its suitability to time, place, and circumstance. Perhaps we ought not to be too severe if a young man verging on manhood seem to spend undue care upon his person; something may be forgiven him, provided he does not carry his foible into the more serious years of life.[1]

26. Selections from Leonardo Bruni's *De Studiis et Literis*. Woodward, *Vittorino da Feltre and other Humanist Educators*, p. 123 ff.

This leads me to press home this truth—though in your case it is unnecessary—that the foundations of all true learning must be laid in the sound and thorough knowledge of Latin: which implies study marked by a

[1] This and the following selections from *Vittorino da Feltre and Other Humanist Educators* by William H. Woodward are used by the courtesy of the Macmillan Company, Publishers, New York.

broad spirit, accurate scholarship, and careful attention to details. Unless this solid basis be secured it is useless to attempt to rear an enduring edifice. Without it the great monuments of literature are unintelligible and the art of composition impossible. To attain this essential knowledge we must never relax our careful attention to the grammar of the language, but perpetually confirm and extend our acquaintance with it until it is thoroughly our own. We may gain much from Servius, Donatus, and Priscian, but more by careful observation in our own reading, in which we must note attentively vocabulary and inflexions, figures of speech and metaphors, and all the devices of style, such as rhythm or antithesis, by which fine taste is exhibited. To this end we must be supremely careful in our choice of authors lest an inartistic and debased style infect our own writing and degrade our taste; which danger is best avoided by bringing a keen, critical sense to bear upon select works, observing the sense of each passage, the structure of the sentence, the force of every word down to the least important particle. In this way our reading reacts directly upon our style.

You may naturally turn first to Christian writers, foremost amongst whom, with marked distinction, stands Lactantius, by common consent the finest stylist of the post-classical period. Especially do I commend to your study his works, *"Adversus falsam Religionem," "De via Dei,"* and *"De opificio hominis."* After Lactantius your choice may lie between Augustine, Jerome, Ambrose, and Cyprian. Should you desire to read Gregory of Nazianzen, Chrysostom, and Basil (*all of them Greeks*), be careful as to the accuracy of the translations you adopt. Of the classical authors Cicero will be your constant pleasure. How unapproachable in wealth of ideas and of language, in force of style, indeed, in all that can attract in a writer! Next to him ranks Virgil, the glory and the delight of our national literature (*to the humanist Latin was part of the Italian tradition*). Livy and Sallust, and then the chief poets, follow in order. The usage of these authors will serve you as your test of correctness in choice of vocabulary and of constructions.

.   .   .   .

What disciplines then are properly open to her (*i. e., to woman*)? In the first place she has before her, as a subject peculiarly her own, the whole field of religion and morals. The literature of the Church will thus claim her earnest study. Such a writer, for instance, as St. Augustine affords her the fullest scope for reverent yet learned inquiry. Her devotional instinct may lead her to value the help and consolation of holy men now living; but in this case let her not for an instant yield to the impulse to look into their writings, which, compared with those of Augustine, are utterly destitute of sound and melodious style and seem to me to have no attraction whatever.

Moreover, the cultivated Christian lady has no need in the study of this weighty subject to confine herself to ecclesiastical writers. Morals, indeed, have been treated by the noblest intellects of Greece and Rome. What they have left to us upon continence, temperance, modesty, justice, courage, greatness of soul, demands your sincere respect. You must enter into such questions as the sufficiency of virtue to happiness; or whether, if happiness consist in virtue, it can be destroyed by torture, imprisonment or exile; whether, admitting that these may prevent a man from being happy, they can be further said to make him miserable. Again, does happiness consist (with Epicurus) in the presence of pleasure and the absence of pain; or (with Xenophon) in the consciousness of uprightness; or (with Aristotle) in the practice of virtue? These inquiries are, of all others, most worthy to be pursued by men and women alike; they are fit material for formal discussion and for literary exercise. Let religion and morals, therefore, hold the first place in the education of a Christian lady.

But we must not forget that true distinction is to be gained by a wide and varied range of such studies as conduce to the profitable enjoyment of life, in which, however, we must observe due proportion in the attention and time we devote to them.

First amongst such studies I place history: a subject which must not on any account be neglected by one who aspires to true cultivation. For it is our duty to understand the origins of our own history and its development, and the achievements of peoples and of kings.

For the careful study of the past enlarges our foresight in contemporary affairs and affords to citizens and to monarchs lessons of incitement or warning in the ordering of public policy. From history, also, we draw our store of examples of moral precepts.

．　　．　　．　　．　　．　　．　　．　　．

To sum up what I have endeavored to set forth. That high standard of education to which I referred at the outset is only to be reached by one who has seen many things and read much. Poet, orator, historian, and the rest, all must be studied, each must contribute a share. Our learning thus becomes full, ready, varied and elegant, available for action or for discourse in all subjects. But to enable us to make effectual use of what we know we must add to our knowledge the power of expression. These two sides of learning, indeed, should not be separated: they afford mutual aid and distinction. Proficiency in literary form, not accompanied by broad acquaintance with facts and truths, is a barren attainment; whilst information, however vast, which lacks all grace of expression, would seem to be put under a bushel or partly thrown away. Indeed, one may fairly ask what advantage it is to possess profound and varied learning if one cannot convey it in language worthy of the subject. Where, however, this double capacity exists—breadth of learning and grace of style—we allow the highest title to distinction and to abiding fame. If we review the great names of ancient literature, Plato, Democritus, Aristotle, Theophrastus, Varro, Cicero, Seneca, Augustine, Jerome, Lactantius, we shall find it hard to say whether we admire more their attainments or their literary power.

But my last word must be this. The intelligence that aspires to the best must aim at both. In doing so, all sources of profitable learning will in due proportion claim your study. None have more urgent claim than the subjects and authors which treat of religion and of our duties in the world; and it is because they assist and illustrate these religious studies that I press upon your attention also the works of the most approved poets, historians, and orators of the past.

27. Selections from Aeneas Silvius Piccolomini's *De Liberorum Educatione*. Woodward, *Vittorino da Feltre,* p. 136 ff.

As regards a boy's physical training, we must bear in mind that we aim at implanting habits which will prove beneficial during life. So let him cultivate a certain hardness which rejects excess of sleep and idleness in all its forms. Habits of indulgence, such as the luxury of soft beds or the wearing of silk instead of linen next the skin, tend to enervate both body and mind. Too much importance can hardly be attached to right bearing and gesture. Childish habits of playing with the lips and features should be early controlled. A boy should be taught to hold his head erect, to look straight and fearlessly before him, and to bear himself with dignity, whether walking, standing, or sitting. In ancient Greece we find that both philosophers and men of affairs— Socrates, for instance, and Chrysippus, or Philip of Macedon—deemed this matter worthy of their concern, and therefore it may well be thought deserving of ours. Games and exercises which develop the muscular activities and the general carriage of the person should be encouraged by every teacher. For such physical training not only cultivates grace of attitude, but secures the healthy play of our bodily organs and establishes the constitution.

Every youth destined to exalted position should further be trained in military exercises. It will be your destiny to defend Christendom against the Turk (*the writer is addressing the youthful king of Hungary*). It will thus be an essential part of your education that you be early taught the use of the bow, of the sling, and of the spear; that you drive, ride, leap, and swim. These are honorable accomplishments in every one and therefore not unworthy of the educator's care. . . .

In respect of eating and drinking, the rule of moderation consists in rejecting anything which needlessly taxes digestion and so impairs mental activity. At the same time fastidiousness must not be humored. A boy, for instance, whose lot it may be to face life in the camp or in the forest, should so discipline his appetite that he may eat even beef. The aim of eating is to strengthen the frame; so let vigorous health reject cakes or sweets, elaborate dishes or small birds or eels, which are for the delicate and the weakly. Your own countrymen, like all northern peoples, are, I know, sore offenders in this matter of eating and drinking. But I count upon your own innate self-respect to preserve you from such bad example and to enable you to despise the sneers and complaints of those around you. What but disease and decay can result from appetite habitually overindulged? To the Greeks of the best age eating and drinking were only means to living, not the chief end and aim of it. For they recognized, with Aristotle, that in this capacity for bodily pleasures we are on the same level with lower creatures. . . .

We must now hasten on to the larger and more important division of our subject, that which treats of the most precious of all human endowments, the mind. Birth, wealth, fame, health, vigor, and beauty are, indeed, highly prized by mankind, but they are one and all of the nature of accidents; they come and they go. But the riches of the mind are a stable possession, unassailable by fortune, calumny, or time. . . .

Need I, then, impress upon you the importance of the study of philosophy and of literature, without which latter indeed philosophy itself is barely intelligible? By this two-fold wisdom a prince is trained to understand the laws of God and of man; by it we are, one and all, enlightened to see the realities of the world around us. Literature is our guide to the true meaning of the past, to a right estimate of the present, to a sound forecast of the future. Where letters cease, darkness covers the land. And a prince who cannot read the lessons of history is a helpless prey of flattery and intrigue.

Next we ask, at what age should a boy begin the study of letters? Theodosius and Eratosthenes regarded the seventh year as the earliest reasonable period. But

Aristophanes, followed by Chrysippus and Quintilian, would have children from the very cradle begin their training under nurses of skilled intelligence. In this matter of nurses the greatest care is necessary, so subtle are the influences which affect the growing mind. But above all other safeguards stands the unconscious guidance of the mother, who, like Cornelia of old, must instil by example a refined habit of speech and bearing.

In religion I may assume from your Christian nurture that you have learnt the Lord's Prayer, the Salutation of the Blessed Virgin, the Creed, the Gospel of St. John, and certain Collects. You have been taught in what consist the chief commandments of God, the gifts of the Spirit, the deadly sins, the way of salvation, and the doctrine of the life of the world to come. This latter truth was, indeed, taught by Socrates, as we know from Cicero. Nor can any earthly interest have so urgent a claim upon us. We should not value this human existence which has been bestowed upon us except in so far as it prepares us for the future state. The fuller truth concerning this great doctrine is beyond your years; but you may, as time goes on, refer to what has been laid down by the great doctors of the Church. And not only by them, for, as Basil allows, the poets and other authors of antiquity are saturated with the same faith and for this reason deserve our study. Literature, indeed, is ever holding forth to us the lesson: "God before all else." As a prince, moreover, your whole life and character should be marked by gratitude for favors showered upon you for no merit of your own, and by reverence, which, in all that concerns the services, the faith, and the authority of the Church, will lead you to emulate the filial obedience of Constantine and Theodosius. For although the priesthood is committed to the protection of kings, it is not under their authority.

(*When the writer penned this sentence, he was already a bishop, but not yet pope.*)

But further: we must learn to express ourselves with distinction, with style and manner worthy of our subject. In a word, eloquence is a prime accomplishment in one immersed in affairs. Ulysses, though a poor warrior, was adjudged worthy of the arms of Achilles by virtue of his persuasive speech. Cicero, too, admonishes us to the same effect: "Let arms to the toga yield." But speech should ever follow upon reflection; without that let a boy, nay, a man also, be assured that silence is the wiser part. Such orators as Pericles and Demosthenes refused to address the Assembly without opportunity for careful preparation. A facile orator speaks from his lips, not from his heart or understanding, and forgets that loquacity is not the same as eloquence. The entire word must in every case be uttered, proper value given to each syllable and each letter, with especial attention to the final sound. Words must not, as it were, linger in the throat, but be clearly emitted, both tongue and lips taking duly their respective parts. . . .

Nature and circumstances thus provide us with the general material of speech, its topics, and broader conditions of their treatment. When, however, speech is considered as an art, we find that it is the function of grammar to order its expression; of dialectic to give it point; of rhetoric to illustrate it; of philosophy to perfect it. But before entering upon this in detail we must first insist upon the overwhelming importance of memory, which is in truth the first condition of capacity for letters. A boy should learn without effort, retain with accuracy, and reproduce easily. Rightly is memory called "the nursing mother of learning." (*The remainder of the treatise is devoted to the elaboration of the elements of his curriculum as here given, that is, of grammar, dialectic, rhetoric, and philosophy.*)

28. Selections from Battista Guarino's *De Ordine Docendi et Studendi*. Woodward, *Vittorino da Feltre and other Humanist Educators*, p. 161 ff.

In offering this short treatise for your acceptance, I am fully aware that you need no incentive to regard the pursuit of letters as the most worthy object of your ambition. But you may find what I have written a not unwelcome reminder of our past intercourse, whilst it may prove of use to other readers into whose hands it may fall. For I have had in view not only students anxious for guidance in their private reading, but masters in search of some definite principles of method in teaching the classics. Hence I have treated both of Greek and of Latin letters and am confident that the course I have laid down will prove a thoroughly satisfactory training in literature and scholarship. I should remind you that the conclusions presented in this little work are not the result of my own experience only. It is indeed a summary of the theory and practice of several scholars, and especially does it represent the doctrine of my father, Guarino of Verona; so much so, that you may suppose him to be writing to you by my pen and giving you the fruit of his long and ripe experience in teaching. May I hope that you will yourself prove to be one more example of the high worth of his precepts?

Let me, at the outset, begin with a caution. No master can endow a careless and indifferent nature with the true passion for learning. That a young man must acquire for himself. But once the taste begins to develop, then in Ovid's words "the more we drink, the more we thirst."

For when the mind has begun to enjoy the pleasures of learning, the passion for fuller and deeper knowledge will grow from day to day. But there can be no proficiency in studies unless there be first the desire to excel. Wherefore let a young man set forward eagerly in quest of those true, honourable, and enduring treasures of the mind which neither disease nor death has power to destroy. Riches, which adventurers seek by land and sea, too often win men to pleasure rather than to learning; for self-indulgence is a snare from whose enticements it is the bounden duty of parents to wean their children, by kind words, or by severity if need arise. Perchance then in later years the echo of a father's wise advice may linger and may avail in the hour of temptation.

. . . .

As regards the course of study. From the first, stress must be laid upon distinct and sustained enunciation, both in speaking and in reading. But at the same time utterance must be perfectly natural; if affected or exaggerated the effect is unpleasing. The foundation of education must be laid in grammar. Unless this be thoroughly learnt, subsequent progress is uncertain—a house built upon treacherous ground.

. . . .

Now these rules can be most satisfactorily learnt from the Compendium written by my father which briefly sets out the more important laws of composition. In using this or a similar text-book the pupil must be practised both in written and in oral exercises. Only by rapid practice in oral composition can fluency and readiness be gained. And this will be further secured if the class is accustomed to speak in Latin.

. . . .

I have said that ability to write Latin verse is one of

the essential marks of an educated person. I wish now to indicate a second, which is of at least equal importance, namely, familiarity with the language and literature of Greece. The time has come when we must speak with no uncertain voice upon this vital requirement of scholarship. I am well aware that those who are ignorant of the Greek tongue decry its necessity for reasons which are sufficiently evident. But I can allow no doubt to remain as to my own conviction that, without a knowledge of Greek, Latin scholarship itself is, in any real sense, impossible.

. . . .

But whilst a beginning is being thus made with Greek, continued progress must at the same time be secured in Latin. For instance, the broader rules of grammar which sufficed in the earlier stages must give place to a more complete study of structure, such as we find in Priscian; and irregularities or exceptions, hitherto ignored, must be duly noted. At the same time the *Letters* of Cicero should be taken in hand for purposes of declamation. Committed to memory they serve as one of the finest possible aids to purity, directness, and facility of style, and supply admirable matter in no less admirable form for adaptation to our own uses. Yet I would not be understood to claim the *Letters* of Cicero as alone offering a sufficient training in style. For distinction of style is the fruit of a far wider field of study. To quote Horace:

Of writing well, be sure, the secret lies
In wisdom: therefore study to be wise.

But we are now passing from the first, or elementary, to the second, or more advanced, stage of grammar which I called historical and which is concerned with the study of continuous prose authors, more particularly the historians. Here we begin with a short but comprehensive view of general history, which will include that of the Roman people by such writers as Justin or Valerius Maximus. The latter author is also valuable as affording actual illustrations of virtuous precepts couched in attractive style. The scholar will now devote his attentions to the historians in regular order. By their aid he will learn to understand the manners, laws, and institutions of different types of nations, and will examine the varying fortune of individuals and states, the sources of their success and failure, their strength and their weakness.

.   .   .   .

Side by side with the study of history a careful reading of the poets will be taken in hand. The true significance of poetic fiction will now be appreciated. It consists, as Cicero says, in the exhibition of the realities of our own life under the form of imaginary persons and situations. Thus Jerome could employ Terence in bringing home his exhortations to temperance. Let us not forget that Virgil as a subject of deep and regular study must always stand not first, but alone. Here we have the express authority of Augustine, who urges the supreme claim of the great poet to our life-long companionship. Lucan may perhaps with good reason be postponed to a later stage. Quintilian regarded him as 'the rhetorical poet'; and undoubtedly his poem has much affinity with certain aspects of the forensic art. There is a certain strain of the keen debater in particular portions of his work. So I should advise that Virgil be followed by Statius, whose *Thebais,* fashioned upon the *Aeneid,* will be found easy reading. The *Metamorphoses* of Ovid form a useful introduction to the systematic knowledge of mythology—a subject of wide literary application deserving close attention.

The course of study which I have thus far sketched out will prove an admirable preparation for that further branch of scholarship which constitutes rhetoric, including the thorough examination of the great monuments of eloquence. The first work to claim our attention in this subject is the *Rhetoric* of Cicero, in which we find all the points of oratory concisely but comprehensively set forth. The other rhetorical writings of Cicero will follow; and the principles therein laid down must be examined in the light of his own speeches. Indeed the student of eloquence must have his Cicero constantly in his hand; the simplicity, the lofty moral standard, the practical temper of his writings render them a peculiarly noble training for the public speaker. Nor should the admirable Quintilian be neglected in this same connection.

It will be desirable also to include the elements of logic in our course of studies, and therewith the *Ethics* of Aristotle and the *Dialogues* of Plato. For these are necessary aids to the proper understanding of Cicero.

.   .   .   .

Before I bring this short treatise to a close I would urge you to consider the function of letters as an adornment of leisure. Cicero, as you may remember, declares learning to be the inspiration of youth, the delight of age, the ornament of happy fortunes, the solace of adversity. A recreation in the study, abroad it is no hindrance. In our work, in our leisure, whether we keep vigil or whether we court sleep, letters are ever at hand as our surest resource. Do we seek refreshment for our minds? Where can we find it more happily than in a pursuit which affords alike utility and delight? If others seek recreation in dice, in ball-play, in the theatre, do you seek it in acquiring knowledge. There you will see nothing which you may not admire; you will hear nothing which you would gladly forget. For good books give no offence, call forth no rebuke; they will stir you, but with no empty hopes, no vain fears. Finally, through books, and books alone, will your converse be with the best and greatest, nay, even with the mighty dead themselves.

.   .   .   .

Let us, then, heeding these great names, see to it that we allow not our short working years to pass idly away. To each species of creatures has been allotted a peculiar and instinctive gift. To horses galloping, to birds flying comes naturally. To man only is given the desire to learn. Hence what the Greeks called 'παιδεία', we call 'studia humanitatis.' For learning and training in virtue are peculiar to man; therefore our forefathers summarized as 'humanitas' the pursuits and activities proper to mankind. And no branch of knowledge embraces so wide a range of subjects as that learning which I have here attempted to describe.

I will end as I began. If this little work fulfils, perhaps more than fulfils, the promise which I held out, it is because it does but exhibit that order and method of study which my learned and revered father has followed for so many years in his own school. For as from the Trojan Horse of old the Greek heroes spread over the captured city, so from that famous Academy of my father has proceeded the greater number of those scholars who have carried learning, not merely throughout Italy, but far beyond her borders.

SUGGESTED EXERCISES

1. Make a study of Petrarch's attitude toward Nature.
2. Study the religious attitude of each one of the humanists here quoted and define the degree of his departure from medieval Christianity.
3. Work out the measure in which Petrarch succeeded or failed to harmonize his new views with his inherited outlook.
4. Establish the stages by which the Greek language and literature captured a permanent place in the training of an educated man.
5. What elements of the curriculum (*trivium, quadrivium*) did the conservatives particularly defend against the innovators (the humanists) and why?
6. When and why was the document, known as the Donation of Constantine, forged and how successful was Valla in his attempt to prove it a forgery?
7. Write a history of book-collection culminating in the great libraries of Pope Nicholas V and Cosimo de' Medici.
8. The place of science (a) in the medieval curriculum, and (b) in the literary curriculum of the humanists. Did the humanists advance the cause of science?
9. Work out the common educational theory underlying the educational programs of Vergerio, Bruni, Piccolomini, and Guarino.
10. Establish the agreements and the differences in the

matter of the actual curricular studies proposed by the four writers on education.

11. If the medieval attitude may be defined in its totality as unworldly, that is, directed toward heaven and eternity, enumerate on the evidence of this material the various ways in which the humanist attitude became worldly, that is, directed toward the earth and practical human interests.

QUESTIONS

1. Petrarch traveled much and largely from curiosity. Draw up a list of the countries and towns he visited on the basis of the evidence in these letters.

2. Was Petrarch a good, that is, a close and intelligent observer of the human scene?

3. Give the medieval school curriculum as defined by the *trivium* and *quadrivium*.

4. What was Petrarch's attitude toward logic (dialectic)?

5. Was Petrarch an uncritical admirer of antiquity?

6. Did Petrarch know Greek and did he and Boccaccio make any effort to learn it?

7. Did Petrarch have a proper estimate of the importance of Greek literature?

8. How critical was Petrarch of the superstitions and science of his age?

9. Who was Aristotle? Who was Averroes? And why was Petrarch critical, in varying degree, of both?

10. Distinguish carefully between the scholastic ideal of education and the new literary ideal of Petrarch.

11. Reconstruct the main elements of the medieval moral

and religious attitude from the dialogue between Petrarch and St. Augustine.

12. Recount what Boccaccio has to say of the Black Death, its symptoms, the manner in which it spread, the methods adopted to avoid it, etc., and pass judgment on the closeness and sobriety of his powers of observation.

13. Boccaccio and Poggio in their tales criticize the *clergy*. On what grounds?

14. Are they or any of the humanists here cited critical of *Christianity?*

15. Why is Coluccio Salutati's correspondent moved to call Virgil "a lying soothsayer"?

16. On what grounds does Salutati defend Virgil and the other pagan authors?

17. What elements of the curriculum (*trivium, quadrivium*) are in dispute between the medievalists and Salutati?

18. Who was Chrysoloras?

19. How did Bruni respond when the opportunity came to learn Greek?

20. Take such a tale as Poggio's about the priest who buried a pet dog—what inference may be drawn therefrom as to the attitude of the common people toward the higher clergy?

21. Who was Jerome of Prague?

22. What features in Jerome's defense elicit Poggio's admiration?

23. How does Jerome's criticism of the Church as revealed in his reported speech at Constance agree with the criticism contained in Boccaccio's and Poggio's tales?

24. Compare Piccolomini's description of Genoa with Petrarch's description of Cologne and comment

on the development which had taken place in observation and vivacious narrative.

25. Did Piccolomini consider the Genoese to be inclined
to humanism?

26. What does Piccolomini have to say of the status and
morals of women in Genoa?

27. List the territories which the Donation of Constantine purported to transfer to Pope Sylvester.

28. Enumerate the critical devices by means of which
Valla proves the Donation to be spurious.

29. How did it happen that over two hundred people
lost their lives at Rome in 1450?

30. Did indulgences play a part in this jubilee?

31. To what use did Pope Nicholas V put his increased
income?

32. By what measures did Pope Nicholas V gather his
great library?

33 How many volumes did his library reach?

34. What main divisions of literature were represented
in the pope's library?

35. Were the libraries of Pope Nicholas and of Cosimo
de' Medici made up of hand-written or printed
books?

36. How did Vespasiano go about the task of stocking
Cosimo de' Medici's library with books?

37. Work out from Vespasiano's figures how long (ap-
proximately) it took one scribe to finish one volume?

38. Did the libraries of Pope Nicholas and Cosimo de'
Medici agree or differ in their main divisions and
general contents?

39. Would it be fair to say that Vergerio upholds individual excellence as the purpose of a liberal education?

40. How does Vergerio's ideal differ from the medieval ideal as defended by St. Augustine in Petrarch's *Secret?*

41. Enumerate the main elements in Vergerio's program of a liberal education.

42. Vergerio concedes a place to music in his program. Did the medieval curriculum neglect music?

43. In their hot pursuit of literature and philosophy as the goal of education the humanists overlook and neglect science. There is one exception to this rule: who is it?

44. Which of the writers on education stress the importance of physical training?

45. What does the emphasis laid by two of the educators on training in arms indicate as to the social class to which they address themselves?

46. The educational scheme is aristocratic, not popular. In the light of the structure of fifteenth century society may it be called practical?

47. Ought an educated man to have proper regard for his outward appearance?

48. In what respects does Bruni's educational program for women differ from the programs for men laid down by the other writers?

49. Show by comparing Guarino with such older writers as Vergerio and Piccolomini that humanism tended to become technical and narrow.

50. To what extent may the humanists be charged with paganism?

51. Did any of them go so far as to advocate the elimination of the Christian ideal from education?

52. In what sense was Valla an enemy of the pope and in what sense was he not an enemy?